For Augie and Paul

Wild Africa and
A Job To Do

With best wishes

Brian Dawlog

x

Wild Africa and A Job To Do

Brian Dawtrey

CGE Publishing Ltd.

First published in Great Britain by CGE Publishing Ltd.

ISBN 978-1-909061-02-6

Printed and bound by Good News Digital Books, Stevenage

To my beloved wife Cicely Jo without whom this book would have been unthinkable and without her love and courage there would be no story to tell.

Thanks go to my daughter Caroline for her help in getting the text concise and correct in every detail.

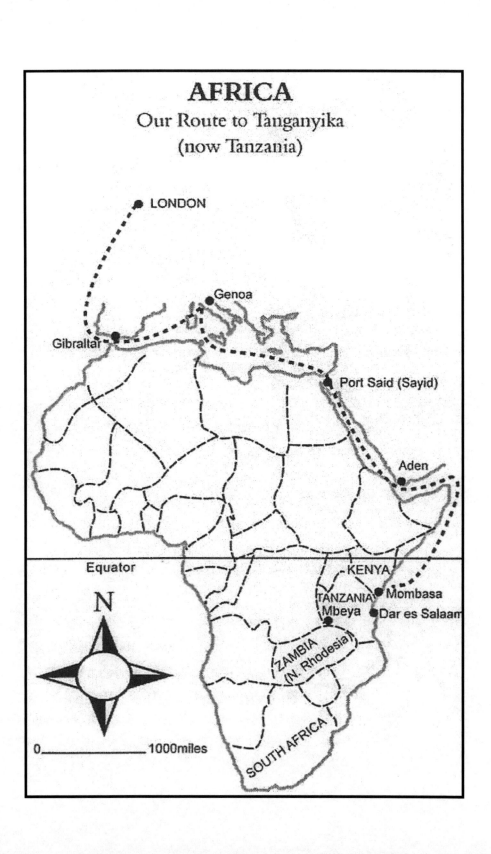

AFRICA
Our Route to Tanganyika
(now Tanzania)

LONDON

Genoa

Gibraltar

Port Said (Sayid)

Aden

Equator

N

KENYA

Mombasa

TANZANIA
Mbeya

Dar es Salaam

ZAMBIA
(N. Rhodesia)

SOUTH AFRICA

0 _____ 1000miles

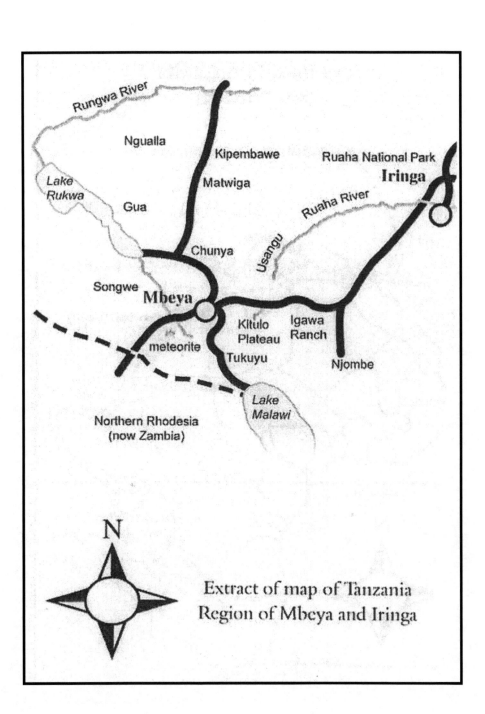

Rungwa River

Ngualla

Kipembawe

Ruaha National Park

Iringa

Matwiga

Lake
Rukwa

Gua

Ruaha River

Usangu

Chunya

Songwe

Mbeya

Kitulo
Plateau

Igawa
Ranch

meteorite

Tukuyu

Njombe

Lake
Malawi

Northern Rhodesia
(now Zambia)

N

Extract of map of Tanzania
Region of Mbeya and Iringa

CONTENTS

Chapter One

Taking The Steamer

As the sun rose on the palm fringed Kenya coast we stood at the rail of *S.S. Kenya Castle* sensing our presence at the brink of a new adventure. We had a wonderful feeling that we had made the right decision. This was the first time in our lives as a young farming family that we had had the time to step back and look at ourselves objectively. We were confident and happy.

My wife Jo looked radiantly beautiful in her summer dress and bronzed skin. Caroline, aged twelve, was a new person, she had become an intelligent socializer, and the boys, aged ten and seven, had learned to swim and collect coins off the bottom of the ship's pool. After three weeks at sea we had learned to look upon the sun, not so much as a holiday deviation but more as a malignant force to be reckoned with. We had learned to roster our exertions in direct ratio to the elevation of the sun, and take salt tablets. We were now tropicalised.

It all began with that fateful decision to do something more worthwhile than managing a farm for a wealthy Norfolk land owner. Departing from the King George V docks at Tilbury on that cold April afternoon of 1962 in the era before jet passenger flight; our goodbyes were seriously meant. Our relations had come down with us on the GWR steam train, feeling that they might never see us again. For them Africa was still the Dark Continent.

We all gathered round a table on board ship for high tea amidst a hubbub of excitement. The ship's Palm Court style orchestra crept into our consciousness with its balmy tranquillising music. Jo and I checked our cabin for the safe arrival of our suit cases and were quite dismayed to find a farewell display of gorgeous flowers from well-wishers. There was one cheerful and practical gift from our brother in law, jovial George, a black rolled umbrella with a gold band.

There was a note which read, 'This is to help you cope with primitive tribes.' I had told George that we would be passing Mount Kilimanjaro where explorer Krapf, in 1848, had encountered a hostile tribe of 'primitive savages bent upon robbing me.' He had resolved that problem by suddenly opening his umbrella towards them, 'with a flourish, frightening them out of their wits'.

Armed with this assertive symbol of British dignity and a contract to serve Tanganyika Government as a Land Planning Officer on a £1200 per year salary, I leaned over the ship's rail and resolutely waved my brolly to our relations below, hoping to raise a smile on their grief stricken faces. The ship's siren blasted its final elephantine call, then over the PA system came the order, 'All ashore that are going ashore', and our umbilical cords were cut.

We headed down the Thames estuary, towards the sun. The ship was designed for the comfort of passengers travelling to the Outposts of Empire, when time was not a pressing feature of travel. Jo remarked that it was like 'travelling backwards in time, to the future.' For the two boys it was a new adventure, freed from their daily morning responsibility of feeding hungry bleating calves before school and for young Philip it was looking after Cinders the donkey. Cinders yawed for a carrot every time he emerged from the barn on his three wheeler. In the evenings it was Philip's job to check that the silky new born baby pigs were all safely snug under the infra-red heaters. For our daughter Caroline, it was more like Alice in Wonderland. But they were all explorers now and the ship's crew would soon get to know of it.

This was the 1960s; society's all-change decade and for us the termination of our happy but impoverished lives as family farmers in favour of taking our chances in newly independent Tanganyika.

Jo and I took refuge from the cold on our cabin beds to ruminate awhile. Would the children miss their happy lives on the farm and their animals? It had been a difficult decision, especially for Jo, who felt her responsibility for keeping our family mentally and physically fit in what she knew would be adverse conditions in Africa. As for myself, I knew that I couldn't go far wrong with my supportive, resourceful and caring wife.

During the next few days we realised that we were different from the other passengers, we were the only complete family, and the only farmers, the rest consisted of newly-weds, singles, missionaries, many colonial civil servants, and military. They were openly sceptical about our status as contractual 'guests' of Tanganyika Government rather than colonial 'ruling elite' and they all freely predicted collapse and chaos in that country. In retrospect, they have been proved wrong. Had they foretold rising poverty they would have been closer to the truth, but there has never been any tribal conflict in what is now Tanzania.

We lapped up the luxury of servants for the three weeks on board ship, and the good fortune of being paid by the British Government to live like aristocracy. The weightiest decisions we had to face were the daily choices of leisure pursuit. We were of a generation that only gained a privilege by toil and sweat. We talked to the missionaries a lot about human motivation in the rural areas of Africa. They invited us to their Kiswahili classes.

On Good Friday we attended the Church of England service. Eighty people attended. It was perhaps symptomatic of the nature of the passengers that The Plate collected £6 as compared to 75p the night before from Bingo.

Our three children were amused by the more stalwart elements of tweed clad Englishmen that daily strode the decks in the face of inclement elements. Caroline said that perhaps sharks that trailed our ship had developed a taste for tweed over the colonial years. The boys did not respond favourably to a nurse running their bath every evening, or to playing the aimless games that had been laid on for their amusement. They instead wormed their way onto the bridge, into the kitchens and the crew's quarters. Caroline told us that the nurse earned £40 per month all found and that there were more crew on the ship than passengers, that we were travelling at 12 knots, and that there was 15,000 feet of water beneath us.

As it grew warmer all port holes were opened so that the lovely sound of ocean accompanied our resting and our dining, along with the ubiquitous mewing of the ship's orchestra. In evening dress at midnight Jo and I strolled amongst the twinkling lights on deck and rededicated our love for each other after fourteen years of marriage. This was to be our unassailable strength in the face of uncertainty.

Gibraltar rock loomed on the horizon and Caroline found out that there were 34 cars to be off loaded by crane into lighters to be ferried into the harbour. One or two Bentley owners were sweating blood and fivers in desperation as their cars hung suspended over the ocean. We took the tender ashore and headed for a taxi to take us up to the free roaming Barbary Apes. We learnt that Barbary was the ancient name of their North African place of origin, so the apes were our first taste of Africa, and they were ready for us. Exploitation was the name of their game. They had benefited from benevolent

3

British rule and like so many colonial subjects, had developed the knack of extracting free food, trinkets, sun glasses, cameras, windscreen wiper blades, ball pens and sympathy from all and sundry white skinned people. Despite a flourish with my rolled umbrella the apes managed to snatch Jo's sun glasses and my Coronet camera.

We were assailed by a loud American from Miami who shot the hackneyed line that we had film star potential, if only he could take a picture of us, a 'so typical British family to show the folks back home.' The children were utterly puzzled. As old wartime Allies, I hailed America with my rolled umbrella raised in salute.

Our next port of call, Genoa, was our first contact with the non-British world. We set off enthusiastically to explore what turned out to be a dingy old city of narrow streets, the sky strewn with washing lines and broken shutters, and instead of the town being steeped in maritime history as we had read, it was steeped in garbage. The only excitement was our taxi which drove round every corner on two wheels. The jabbering driver steered with one hand, his other being fully engaged pressing his hooter as vigorously as the throttle. The noise in the city was horrendous and the coffee 'like tractor sump oil', according to Richard. The star-struck revolver toting policemen in their pluming topes got so excited over trifles, not to mention numerous high heeled tarts toting for business, that the whole scene was more in the nature of a floor show than a maritime business centre. In desperation we tried their British sounding toasted sandwiches. 'Yuk!' was the response to the bacon slices between bread soaked in olive oil. We escaped on the funicular for 100 lira each to the mountain top. It was a joy to feel grass under our feet again, only to find that we had to pay again to get down! We later discovered that the correct fare was 40 lira return. Our opinion of Italy further degenerated.

We were famished by the time we returned to the ship for Richard's 10th birthday tea. It was the twenty sixth of April 1962. He was astonished and overjoyed to get a birthday cake from the Captain. There were cards too and many gifts from the folks back home. Richard still has vivid memories of the unexpected kindness shown to him in that strange place.

The second day in port found us heading for a fishing village called Camogli, 16 miles down the rocky coast by autobus   again on two wheels. There were no cottages like in Cornwall but the ubiquitous blocks of flats, painted in insipid fading colours and festooned with washing lines and fishing nets. The school girls uniformly wore a smock with a neck ribbon and often a showy bonnet with a bob and a tassel. We got on very well with the fishermen, and one took us for a row round the bay for an hour. His language added colour and charm to our image of Camogli.

We gladly left Genoa, as did Columbus, never to return. Sailing south that evening with Stromboli coughing sparks on our left, like a Roman candle, I fell asleep on deck and had a vivid dream about being in charge of a platoon of black corpses who obeyed my orders implicitly and I began screaming in some strange lingo. Jo later declared it to be corrupted half learned Swahili. I recalled panicking when the corpses refused to obey my order to lie down and awoke to find myself surrounded by alarmed passengers who said that I was rolling about squealing like a rat. Was this the portent of things to come in Darkest Africa?

It took immense grit to attend Kiswahili lessons in the Med. The sun drew the irresistible me and the delightful Jo to the pool side in as little as possible for as long as possible. Navel gazing took on a whole new perspective now that the bikini era had taken hold of the girls and the boys. I felt that I had been missing out engrossed in byres and fields seven days a week. Wow! To hell with deck games, when those white bodies needed a Brylcream massage to protect them from the sun, there was no trouble getting them to lie down.

Even before we tied up at Port Sayid the ship was surrounded by traders in colourful rowing boats far below us, laden with goods made from camel skins and brass. They screamed up at us in broken English, 'Hey you! Magregor! Catch my line. Best prices here.' In no time the deck was humming with business, and small Arab boys were diving to the sea bed for coins, oblivious of the oil discharge from the ship.

The crew were full of stories about Arabs kidnapping children and passengers being knifed despite there being soldiers everywhere. Egypt was under the wing of Kruschev, President Nasser's friend. The children stayed behind to enjoy the Gulli Gulli Man who was now on board from here to Suez. For gullible passengers, a master of trickery and illusion, inherited they say from his parentage back to 1915 from whence he had learned to keep saluting. Live day old chicks appeared from every part of the children's anatomy amidst great hilarity. He presented the adults with silver looking coins which provoked the opening of purses from which half crowns seem to vanish in disbelief.

Port Sayid turned out to be a traffic free zone though they were contributing to global warming with ankle deep nauseous camel and horse dung. We discussed whether to release the pitifully bleating sheep tied to a tree awaiting its ceremonial Muslim throat cutting, but decided that the soldiery might not appreciate the concept of animal rights. An old man stood near crushing large pupae in a jar for a high protein lunch, another offered us wilted vegetables, and child beggars dressed in tatty pijamas, with an eye or a hand missing, followed us in droves. One made us a heart rending offer of a rose, for a shilling.

We ventured to enter a Community Hall bedecked with portrait posters of Nasser, and the Soviet Red Flag. Inside was an exhibition of the good life in Russia with the ubiquitous Allah replaced by Kruschev. We joined the hundreds of expectant children seated on wooden benches for the film. They had hoped for Cowboys and Indebums but were soon bored by the Bolshoi Ballet.

We emerged to find ourselves amidst a funeral procession of some 80 turbaned moaning mourners, and decided to beat a hasty retreat to British soil.

During our absence Richard and Philip had shown their farmer's boy initiative and done deals, a la Norwich Market, with the Arabs, swapping bowls of ship's fruit for bone broaches, a pair of leather sandals, a camel skin wallet, and a Sudanese *pouffé*.

'Did you get any good deals in town Dad?' enquired Richard, forestalling any queries as to their honesty.

What could I say?

The next day in the Suez Canal was a case of mad dogs and Englishmen go out in the mid-day sun. I called for my black umbrella and joined a couple of Arab gentlemen standing in thick cotton robes and head dress. We chatted coolly by the pool whilst European men around us shed their shirts, cotton fibre versus moral fibre, you might say.

We were now living a life that was changing us. Jo, instead of washing eggs each evening was learning to play golf each evening, with cigarette ends laid on the deck matting. Her tutor was a handsome young Scottish horticulturalist named David. I was relieved to later discover that he was posted to Dar es Salaam, two days drive from Arusha, our posting. Jo challenged him to put a golf ball down the ship's funnel from the afterdeck, thus perpetuating the liaison.

Evening strolls were now accompanied by barking canal frogs, hugely fat on gorged grass hoppers that struck the ship's lights and fell, barbecued in their own fat.

We woke at dawn to find ourselves in a sea of blue ink, backed by blood red hills. Shoals of little silver flying fish raced ahead of us. Probably they enjoyed escaping the hot sea water, which Caroline advised us, was 86 degrees farenheit. Despite the heat we were still being served four course breakfasts, six course lunches, eight course dinners, not to mention afternoon tea! We felt that we should pluck up the courage to miss a meal. Our dislike for a new table companion named Edna encouraged us to do so.

After lamenting the 'appalling lack of classes on this ship' Edna continued, 'I've lived in Dar es Salaam for nine years by the way, hope you're not going there, awful place, lizard droppings on the furniture, nothing for teenagers to do, and the humidity! God it's terrible, your clothes rot in the wardrobes and you need a cold shower three times a day. The air smells morbid too; I think it's the bats that fly up and down the passageways in my house. And the lettuces, don't eat the lettuces my dears, there's amoebic dysentery in the lettuces. Livingstone died of amoebic dysentery you know, there's still no cure.'

'Did Doctor Livingstone eat lettuces?' asked seven year old Philip; by accident or design I wasn't sure.

'Well no I suppose not,' stumbled Edna.

'I'd say it was most unlikely,' ventured Caroline in her best la-di-da voice, 'lettuces are a temperate climate crop.'

Edna, thankfully, withdrew gracefully.

That evening in the Red Sea we danced under the stars after a cabaret, and David put a golf ball down the ship's chimney. *Kenya Castle* didn't even cough.

After 400 miles in 24 hours we anchored off Steamer Point, Aden. The sea and air temperature had now reached a sweltering 93 degrees. We opted for sleeping on deck instead of under the cabin punka louvers.

After a family conflab we decided to mount our own expedition into town with hats and umbrella. Aden harbour was invitingly green, unlike Port Sayid, fringed with coconut palms and backed by countless duty free shops owned by Indians. We took the launch and browsed the shops. All the technological wonders of the western world were on offer, at rock bottom prices. The tax-free world was a strange unrecognisably comfortable place!

We were befriended by a cute Bedouin girl aged about 10 years, dressed in long cotton patterned clothes and head dress, and abundant beads, bangles and ear rings. She guided us to the statue of Queen Victoria, sitting there regally with her sceptre and with a crow sitting upon her orb, she imperiously gazed seawards towards her beloved India. Over the harbour gateway were still the words, For *King and Empire*.

Our Bedouin girl took us to Crater Town, where the crumbling streets smelled of incense, spice, coffee, wood smoke, and the kitchen smells of garlic and curry. Further down the slope vacant plots attracted sewage.

Many women were in purdah and obviously poor but friendly as were the children. A raggedly dressed group sat round a blackboard diligently scrawling Arabic words from the Koran. Other children were chalking patterns on the horns of their goats, whilst bony cows wandered everywhere amongst the houses, helping themselves to anything they could reach in doorways or amongst cooking pots. We felt sad for the animals.

An old man sat in a doorway chewing betel nuts and spitting red juice through a gap in his front teeth, right across the pavement in front of us.

Caroline grimaced, 'That man's mouth is bleeding. How horrid.'

Into the Indian Ocean, with 12,000 feet of ocean beneath us, we crossed the Equator. King Neptune himself reared his fearful, seaweed entangled crown and was hauled aboard to hold court on the afterdeck. We all gathered round the pool to witness the maritime drama. It was a highly colourful ceremony. Leading members of the ship's company were called to answer charges of misconduct with certain passengers. The sentence was to have certain vital organs removed by carving knife; the resultant sea of blood was then assuaged by a ducking in the pool. As in the Middle Ages, a good time was had by all.

After those grim proceedings, the evening found us all hanging over the rail gazing down at the heaving black bottomless depths, thinking how easy it would be for a person to disappear forever, especially at night. Our great ship full of light was suddenly a star in a black universe of death that seemed to claw up at the ship's sides, grasping for any errant child, or suicidal wife.

We all shuddered and headed off for the dining room. The tranquillity of the ship's orchestra still meowing the same old tunes after 5,000 miles seemed almost fun.

One day out from Aden Jo went down with heat stroke and it took a saline drip to get her back on her feet. Richard too had skin blisters and Philip dizzy spells and rashes.

Jo gathered together a group of passengers and they agreed that the crew had been special in the way that they had looked after the children and entertained the passengers. She suggested that with the excellent wardrobe on the ship they could put on a large part of South Pacific before they reached Mombasa. Jo is a charismatic and lovable person and loves nothing more than being herself, with an audience. Her enthusiasm proved infectious and a full cast of passengers soon materialised.

Bloody Mary was played fantastically by a man who had hardly spoken to a soul on board. Putting on a black wig had turned him into another person. The show was a great success with Jo as the producer. The captain said that such an event had never occurred before in the history of *Kenya Castle*.

Suddenly it was the twelfth of May and ship talk was only of Kenya. We gathered at the ship's rail and gazed at the approaching ancient and mysterious coastline wondering was The Interior really a Dark Continent?

Chapter Two

East African Railways and Harbours

Impatient to set foot in Africa Jo was one of the first down the gang plank in Mombasa. She stood on the colourful sun baked quay looking up at the two boys and me leaning on the ship's rail awaiting Caroline. Twelve and three quarter years old; every quarter counts at her age; blonde, sun tanned, Caroline, was attracting intense interest from the crew, both black and white and loving every minute of it. Our sadness at ending such an eventful voyage of three weeks, seeming more like three months, was tempered by the sudden impact of stepping into another world. From the bleak ocean we had been pitched into a cosy welcoming atmosphere of balmy heat, swaying palms and mellow deep velvety African voices, 'Jambo Bwana. Jambo watoto wa Uliya. Tunapende Wazungu.' Meaning, 'Hello Bwana. Hello children of Europe. We like white people.'

Bright sun seems to invite a display of colour, ladies dresses, flowering shrubs, brilliant hovering sun birds, large orange and blue lizards, lurking on the rocks and walls, the Union Jack fluttering under a deep blue sky above the tin customs shed. A heady scent of frangipani pervaded the air.

The Government Coastal Agent, an Asian, stood out in his immaculate white uniform amongst the mêlée of Kenyan and English women on the quay in their light summer dresses, excitedly awaited the passengers as they trooped down the gang plank. His ego aglow, the Coastal Agent was soon in full attendance upon the charming Jo in her broad brimmed hat and a flowing full skirted cotton dress, looked the picture of cool calm English beauty as she waved a beckoning white gloved hand to us. I became excited seeing her as

I'd never seen her before, thankful that she was my lady.

My imagination slipped back in credulity to our Norfolk fields and that lithe figure in corduroys and check shirt, bouncing on the seat of our grey Fergy tractor, knocking the last clods into user-friendly crumbs in readiness for this year's spring malting barley seed. Was this the same Jo of the one thousand barn hens? The same Jo that, after cooking supper for the family, drove out all over the county in our old Land Rover teaching Keep-Fit for the Norfolk Education Committee so that she could save up enough money to buy that wonderful new invention, a Hoover washing machine?

The Coastal Agent was bursting with valuable information, guidance and assurances of his competence in handling our twenty crates of household effects, including that valuable piece of modern technology Jo's new Hoover washing machine.

'Not to worry Mrs Dawtrey. Your crates will be on that train. Don't give it a second's thought. You've got four days in Mombasa before the train goes and you've got a sleeper compartment already booked to Arusha in Tanganyika. So relax and enjoy yourselves. I suggest the Nyali Beach Hotel. I've hired a car for you. It's over there. Pay the driver twenty five shillings, no more. I do hope we shall meet again, perhaps in the hotel bar this evening? I'll drop in about eight.'

'Brian. It seems like we've slipped back a generation don't you think? We've been waited on hand and foot since we left London. I like it. I feel as though I'm, somebody.'

'And you certainly look, *somebody*, doesn't she Caroline?'

We talked in the taxi.

'It seems like years since we left Home Farm, and our animals. We are not family farmers any more. I am now referred to as a government officer. I've only to raise my hand and someone rushes to pick up my bag.'

'Yes ... Sir!' rejoined Philip with a mocking salute, 'Dad? Do you think Lassie and her pups will be okay while we're away?'

Our African driver had plenty to say about what a wonderful country Kenya was and how he hoped we'd have a great time and perhaps decide to stay permanently. He treated us like his personal guests. We soon discovered that this was typical African hospitality.

The shear abundance of mangoes burdening the trees along the route to town seemed almost too daunting a prospect for pickers and no one bothered.

The hot crowded main street was a riot of colourful Asian ladies in saris and traders stalls, heaving under the weight of wooden carvings, trophy ivory, zebra and antelope skins, tropical shells from the coral reefs nearby, and intricate silver jewellery from Zanzibar. We learned that the source of pure silver was 1780 Marie Theresia coins, once the currency of East Africa. Islamic architecture reminded us of Mombasa's long history of Arabic domination. No African had ever ruled this coast.

The hotel reception treated us as seasoned world travellers, accustomed to the highest standards of cuisine. Little did they know that we had never before experienced such exotically beautiful surroundings and lavish comforts. Our suit cases disappeared and we 'took tea' beside the sparklingly blue swimming pool. Beyond the pool spread deserted white coral beaches quietly lapped by the unhurried waves of an azure sea protected by distant coral reefs. There was some talk by the waiters of government plans to make their coast a holiday resort for international tourists. We thought that there would have to be a quicker way of reaching the place.

'Why didn't someone tell us about Kenya Colony Brian?' Jo said over tea, 'We wouldn't have signed up for Tanganyika, would we? But then I suppose Kenya will be independent too before long.'

In the evening Jo and I strolled along the tide line, hand in hand, bathed in a flood of brilliant moonlight, the caressing breeze catching the fine needles of the Casurarina whispering pines along the shore. There was no one else in our world at that moment; it was as though the trees were whispering to us, why have you been so long in coming?

We all agreed that we would make our whole lives henceforth in Africa.

'We've always wanted to come,' Jo told the children, 'Then the Coronation in 1953 was so wonderful and rationing ended and a new exciting world emerged in England, so we stayed on. We did apply for a job in Uganda in 1956 but the government told us that it was unhealthy for children and dangerous; uncivilized; no doctors and only rain water to drink.'

At dawn the children were out exploring. We had a job to get them back in for breakfast, and then they didn't thank us for that yukki paw-paw, but the eggs and bacon; wow... 'just like home.'

Already perspiring in the coastal humidity we all set off to walk the white coral sands of the Indian Ocean. Residential properties fringed the beach with vast lawns, their open windows inviting the tranquil sound of the surf on the reef, and the heady scent of frangipani and gardenia blossom onto their breakfast tables. We saw several white uniformed house servants waiting at table, and garden boys casually enjoying a good living relieving their employers of toil in the oppressive heat.

'No wonder these folks keep so quiet about their good fortune, they've really got it made, haven't they. I wonder how the Africans do in their villages,' Jo questioned, 'We could hire a car and head out of town along the coast. What do you say?'

'Okay. Let's do that.'

We ferried out to the mainland and were soon bouncing along our first murram road. Tall coconut trees shading villages of mud brick houses. They were waterproofed with folded dried palm leaves called *makuti*. Well dressed African women with gaggles of naked children about them, were sweeping their forecourts bare of loose soil and litter to deter snakes and fire ants. We could see their men folk fishing on the ocean in their ancient lateen-rigged canoes. With their outriggers they looked like the precursors of the modern catamaran. A group of young women still preserving their African grace bare to the waist, prettily tattooed and decorated with wire and beads, waved happily to us.

Instead of flowering shrubs to beautify their surrounds like English villages, these were surrounded by groves of bananas, mangoes, avocados, paw-paw, and lemons. Maize grows all the year round on the coast and the women were rhythmically pounding it in their heavy wooden pestles whilst singing rounds to relieve the monotony, with their latest addition to the family bouncing rhythmically upon their backs.

African villagers appeared to own nothing and did not look upon ownership as a necessary ambition in life. Their viewpoint was that land, and water, was God's territory under the guardianship of the chief, which upon reflection, is exactly what the American Indians always maintained. There was no need of mortgage debts in this society, none of the plagues of obligatory electricity and water bills, and fuel was free. Canoes were carved out of God's tree trunks. The only taxes were those on four wheels that took the men to market to sell their fish, so that they could buy a radio, a paraffin lamp or a cotton vest and long trousers. We decided that we had been misinformed about Africans living in poverty.

Back at the hotel the manager advised us not to be too adventurous.

'Don't go wandering down the back streets of Mombasa, especially in the evening. Dhows are coming in on the monsoon now and their crews are on the lookout for young women, especially white women, whom they can take back to Saudi Arabia and sell for tremendous prices to Arab sheikhs. What's more they never seem to escape. I don't know whether that's because they enjoy the luxury of the harem or that they're too closely guarded?'

'If they try to grab one of us they'll have a fight on their hands I can tell you,' stormed Jo.

We could all vouch for that; a very fiery nature has this tractor driver.

On the last day in Mombasa we extricated the boys from hunting the big blue and yellow lizards that bob up and down behind every large rock and the highly defensive red fiddler crabs on the beach, in favour of an educational tour of Fort Jesus. Their glum faces perked up when they heard talk of Turkish pirates invading the island in 1588.

'The same year as the Armada you know,' quoth Brian at the boys, 'but more successful. They slaughtered the Arab rulers and took over.'

They enjoyed the continuum about the cannibal tribe called Zimba who ate their way up the coast from Zimbabwe to Mombasa, and then ate the Turkish pirates. When you get to know the history, current events seem less inexplicable! We learned that in 1591 the Portuguese arrived and built the fort. The Arabs retaliated in 1696 and besieged the Portuguese in the castle. After two years of terrible suffering the surviving nine surrendered. The following day the Portuguese rescue fleet appeared. The Sultan of Zanzibar then owned Mombasa until the British came in 1824.

The following day our holiday, on half salary, came to a chilling halt with the appearance of a bill on the breakfast table. We couldn't stay here forever after all. No one expressed regrets as we presented ourselves at the Coastal Agency Office.

The Agent advised, 'It's easier to reach Arusha via Mombasa, Kenya, than via Dar es Salaam, the capital of Tanganyika,' So the Dawtrey invasion would be via Taveta which is on a ridge of upland forming the national boundary, between Mount Kilimanjaro and the Pare Mountains.

'Now, are you listening you children?' the Agent continued, 'Before you reach Taveta, the train stops at Voi, in the Tsavo Game Reserve, lots of wild animals there, and then the train divides like a worm chopped in half,' he chuckled, 'one half goes to Nairobi and the other half goes to Arusha. Make sure you get on the Arusha half, okay?'

East African Railways & Harbours or EAR & H, were a vital trading link between Uganda, Kenya and Tanganyika and the rest of the world, built in early colonial times.

There was a pregnant pause as though being Tanganyikans he had lost the incentive to fuss over us.

He ruffled his papers, 'While you wait at Voi you will be the guests of EAR & H, for breakfast. I have booked a First Class compartment for you on the train, your name will be on the door and my driver will take you all down to the station. The train leaves in about an hour. Don't be late though because the driver might take off early if the train is full.'

We occupied our sleeper compartment after we had received absolute assurance from the African Guard that our 20 crates of household effects, including the Hoover washing machine, which we had not seen since Home Farm, were on the train.

'We should not have mentioned twenty,' said Caroline mistrustfully, 'but asked him how many of our crates he had on the train.'

'Hmmm ... you're learning fast Caroline.'

As we steamed out over the bridge from the island to the mainland, the sun was sinking ahead of us. Heavy rain had cooled things off a bit and the journey through the groves and plantations of the coastal belt was most pleasant. About twenty miles out the slow train toiled ever more slowly as we climbed to the African plateau. As we passed through park like scenery we stuck our heads out for a last look back at Mombasa and the twinkling blue sea. We had no idea what lay ahead of us, we all sat quietly gazing out of the window. We were in semi desert type scrub, totally uninhabited, except for two ostriches that stood jauntily staring at us as we passed slowly by, their faces looking like Donald Duck.

By 6.30 pm it was pitch black, just sparks from the chimney and the brightest stars we had ever seen.

'Are they the same stars we had in Norfolk Mum?' enquired Caroline.

'Certainly. Just cleaner air that's all.'

We steamed into Voi station in the small hours. I was immediately awake and apprehensive. The rest snored on. Then the guard began shouting, 'All out! Voi. All out!'

He opened all the doors, slamming them noisily to assert his authority.

'What's going on?' I shouted hoarsely at the departing guard, 'We are all in our pyjamas. What's going on?'

He turned to address us in a slightly more pleading tone, *'All out Bwana. Poli Bwana, ni lazima, kwa sababu ...'*

'He's apologizing,' said Jo remembering her Kiswahili lessons with the missionaries on board ship, 'I'm not sure what he said after "because". That fancy pants coastal agent assured us that we would not have to change trains!'

'We'd better move,' I declared, pulling on some shorts in the half light, 'All the crates are on this train though. I'd better stick with it. You all go. Find the stationmaster and see what he's got to say for himself. Put your sweaters on over your pyjamas, I think it's cold outside. See you on the platform later then.'

In the thin dawn light I could see the stationmaster, a Singh, trying to stave off marauding women and children trembling with rage and cold. There were several men there too, to whom the Singh turned for sympathy,

'That foolish boy! Is always making trouble for me! Oh dear, oh dear, oh dear. I am ever so very sorry, sirs. There is ever so plenty time please, yes. You can all get dressed and go down to the hotel for breakfast. No problem please. We pay!'

'I wish we were back on the farm,' moaned Richard over the breakfast table, 'this paw-paw is god awful, tastes like tractor paraffin.'

Back on the platform the darkness added gloom to despondency as everyone climbed back into the train, pondering whether this half might go on to Nairobi after all. No one seemed to be sure. Reassuringly, our names were still on the door.

'Jo, I'll have another go at the stationmaster. You wait here with the children.' I said.

He was not in his office. I went to the forecourt and found the guard blithely ignoring a tirade of staccato rapid fire Swahili from the turbaned, furious, head bobbing stationmaster. The guard took the opportunity to vanish when I spoke.

'Excuse me. Do we have to change trains to go to Arusha?'

'Goodness gracious, no. We are only waiting for the down train to pass. That is all.'

I returned to the platform in time to see our train and my wife and family disappearing down the track towards Nairobi ...

'My God!' I turned to the guard who emerged by my side.

'You fool! Why didn't you tell me it was due to leave?' I railed at the guard, feeling some sympathy with the Singh, 'Now what am I going to do? I have to go to Tanganyika not Kenya.'

'Oh .... you want go Tanganyika. Ah ... good place. You like there. Ah .... sorry for er .... er .... delay!'

'I am annoyed with you, you understand, I am going to tell the station master, you are an idiot.'

'Oh, he knows, ... everything Bwana. *Sijambo Bwana. Itarudi tena.*'

I knew that *itarudi* meant it will return. But when? After it's been to Nairobi? Of course, it always does! The guard's right, it's me that's stupid, of course, this is Africa after all. I thought I'd go and have another chat with the stationmaster anyway; it would pass the time, for two or three days?

I burst into his office, 'Not to worry Bwana.'

Where had I heard that before!

'It go siding, a quarter mile, only, Sir. Everything under control Sir, not to worry please.'

I found a seat on the platform and sat, trying to cultivate an African outlook. The seat struck cold against my bare legs. As the morning mist swirled across the steel track my mind returned to those terrifying tales that I had read about on board ship. This was that very spot, Voi, when the line was under construction in 1900, that the horror occurred.

It all came flooding back, I was filled with apprehension. Those phrases, 'swirling mist', 'whooping hyenas', 'man-eating lions' lurking in the bush, their yellow eyes 'like two very bright glow worms in the darkness, sprang to life. The story was that the superintendent had 'heard about the workers being killed by lions' and had come to inspect the security arrangements at Voi station. He had decided to occupy a carriage in that very siding where Jo and the children were said to be now, with his colleagues and a rifle. The word was that 'the brute was daring and showed no racial or class discrimination in its tastes except that it had an extraordinary appetite for railway people'.

The story went that the guard dozed off, the lion mounted the carriage by the rear platform, reached the sliding door which was on brass runners, knocked it aside and entered the sleeping compartment. The lion then grabbed the sleeping superintendent by the shoulder and attempted to leave, but the sliding door had closed due to a slight tilt of the carriage and the lion jumped out through the side window, doing much damage to the carriage and the superintendent. Lumps of flesh and bone were found a quarter of a mile away the next day. The head was separate being inedible, the eyes still glaring in terror.

History was repeating itself; I could hear hyenas whooping and the distant growl of lion. Sure enough there was something approaching along the track in the mist.

Chapter Three

UHURU

The mist parted to reveal, not a lion, but people carrying bags.

I shouted, 'Hi .... hurry, there are lions about.'

I was panicking, possessed, 'No .... sorry, it's okay, take your time. They've gone.'

I suddenly realised that it was Jo and the three children. We embraced on the platform trembling and silent, except that is for Jo who was never down but furious. She was all keyed up to express herself in terrifying staccato tones.

'This bloody EAR & H, is a crazy organisation. They couldn't organise a piss up in a brewery.'

Where had I heard that before? Ah yes about the Norfolk Education Committee.

'I'm going to kill that silly nodding turbaned stationmaster. I'll bet my Hoover's gone to Nairobi! Right I'm off to see that Singh. He'll sing before I've finished with him, mark my words.'

'Jo just hang on. There's something moving in the mist... looks like a carriage.... it's our carriage... it's coming back to pick us up.'

'Brian. If you think I'm going to get back on that train then you don't know me!'

After another turban wobbling exchange we all silently re-entered the carriage marked Dawtrey family and continued our journey to Tanganyika.

With steam up, and sun up, Kilimanjaro glisteningly filled our window, a stunning sight. We all burst into peals of laughter.

'Here endeth the first lesson in culture shock!' rounded Jo.

Travel in Comfort was not one of the slogans of EAR & H, neither was punctuality, or speed; we rarely achieved 30 mph. We climbed slowly through the broad gap in the mountain ranges, leaving behind us in the rain shadow of the greatest mountain in Africa, the dry wild animal side of Kilimanjaro. The point where the rains of the south side began was called Taveta. From there on the scene became ever greener, an agricultural landscape with people replacing wild animals. This used to be the German side. They introduced sisal from Mexico in 1893 and we were now surrounded by it.

Five foot long hideous spears of thick leathery leaves marched away in military lines of sameness as far as the eye could see, not a weed, not a bird, not a tree, a desert of sisal. Tanganyika was notable then as the world's biggest exporter of sisal.

I had never seen sisal before and said, 'Look at that kids, pineapples.'

The ignorance of a new born aid worker! I would never live that down. Every time we saw pineapples in the market I knew what was coming.

'Will it be sisal for Sunday lunch then Dad? '

A famous German named Krupp invented a decorticating machine powerful enough to crush sisal leaves and extract the 95% green water leaving the white fibre to bleach in the sun ready for making ropes and mats. The Germans were masters at marshalling the slave labour needed for the gruelling work of cutting sisal leaves and loading them onto train wagons to go to the decorticator. By all accounts, the principle incentive for the African worker at the time was the *kiboko*, a hippo hide whip.

The tribe in those parts are Wachagga. They dwell around Moshi town in the foothills of the mountain, and are traditionally very good farmers, growing coffee and fattening cattle in boxes. In 1884 the explorer Johnston wrote to the British Government about the high intelligence of the Wachagga and their sophisticated irrigation farming system.

He wrote, '…. the people of Moshi would welcome British rule.' Unfortunately the Germans beat them to it.

Once over the shoulder of Kilimanjaro we ran down hill at such a pace that I feared the train would jump off the rails. Sisal gave way to lush gardens, and elephant grass six foot tall.

'They didn't invent the lawn mower here did they!' was Richard's comic comment.

Moshi looked modern and prosperous despite its rusting corrugated iron roofs, the biggest building being the Moshi Coffee Growers Co operative. As we came into the station small African boys clambered on the carriage doors thrusting their wares through the windows, principally bananas, oranges, guavas, cooked groundnuts, and Coca Cola. One or two smaller boys fell onto the track, causing great hilarity amongst their 'survival of the fittest' competitors.

The train now turned westwards with Kilimanjaro on our right and distant Arusha marked on the skyline by another volcano called Meru, about fifty miles further on.

Terminally we checked in at Arusha Railway Hotel, a spreading single story building with delightful grounds, refreshingly green after the rainy season and with 4,000 foot altitude coolness. It had taken us four weeks to reach our Station, a journey that today takes tourists twelve hours.

Tengeru Agricultural Research Station was a few miles out of town, and this was to be our home from now on. The Senior Research Officer, Dr Van Rensburgh, and his wife, gave us a warm welcome and introduced us to several Canadian and British families living in this pleasantly verdant location. So far we were delighted.

Our government quarter was a little red brick house which had been occupied by an African family with consequential fleas, muddy floors, smoke smelling rooms and overgrown extensive garden. It was, as we were told, on its way, meaning back to bush. We were astonished to find our twenty crates in the driveway. We all agreed that it was a miracle of Asian ingenuity.

In the house was a Dover stove for cooking, or kuni stove which is Swahili for wood. There was electric light but no power plugs for the Hoover washing machine.

Jo was shattered, 'All those months of teaching evening classes on cold winter nights .... Wasted. They say anticipation is always the best part of acquisition.'

Richard sympathetically added, 'Mrs Van Rensburgh says we should buy a paraffin powered fridge, couldn't we get a paraffin powered washing machine?'

'You stupid boy!' reacted Jo, getting increasingly annoyed with our whole situation, 'And do you know what that Mrs Van Rensburgh said to me this morning. Do I play tennis? As if I had nothing better to do than play tennis, I ask you.'

Of course Mrs Van Rensburgh was right; tennis was a healthy way of relating to the expatriate community and sharing frustrations. She did say we should get a houseboy straight away, and she would send some candidates round. Jo was now faced with the monumental challenge of creating a home. Furthermore she was going to have to do it on her own, for I had still to tell her that I was already instructed by the Director of Research to go on a ten day safari the next day. Land Planning Officer Bill Bell, from whom I was to take over, was overdue for leave and had a distant safari planned for us.

The garden was only too obviously infested with poisonous snakes and mosquitoes. Caroline had already found a cobra curled up between her feet when reaching for oranges in the long grass. She stood petrified as it slid away harmlessly. I was concerned for Jo and the children facing this 'baptism of fire' during my absence, as Jo put it, 'swanning about the countryside'. She was further dismayed by what she met in the kitchen, that image of an English lady standing on the quay in a hat, gloves and rustling cotton skirt with everyone anxious to wait upon her, was horribly submerged in a swarm well fed rustling cockroaches.

The children however were excitedly exploring every corner of the garden.

'Brian, get those children in!' Jo was panicking with frustration.

The three of them appeared round the corner of the house all smiles, carrying the biggest banana leaves in all Africa, they said, certainly six feet tall. I took their photograph. They had been playing Pooh sticks; dropping marked grapefruits at the top end of the water furrow and racing down to the bottom to catch the first one home. Caroline declared as knowingly as ever;

'The Garden of Eden must have been like this Dad; there are grapefruit trees, guavas, oranges and water furrows.'

Being near to Dr Leakey's Cradle of Mankind, Olduvai Gorge, Caroline had a point, 'All we need is a Boy to cut the grass.' she concluded.

The best thing I could think of for Jo was to take her to tea with the other ladies on the Research Station, and leave our crates until morning. Bill would have to wait until lunch time. The other wives were highly organized and very comfortable with servants running around enjoying the employment. We were found guest beds for the night. Such a kind and generous atmosphere seems to be the norm in many such isolated communities. We were offered help to find a cook and a shamba boy.

In the morning Jo was, thankfully, her old industrious self. We had electric light but no power. When we married just after the war we didn't have electricity or mains water in our rural pre-fabricated bungalow and so to us the dreaded black kuni stove didn't look quite so black in the daylight.

A potential cook appeared on our doorstep. He was small with a big name, Samson. He said that he had always cooked with *kuni*, Samson Emily was a tonic at that moment; he made us all laugh, demonstrating his culinary skills by clowning about. He was a local Mchagga and apparently his mother had aspirations for her new-born to grow mightily powerful like Kilimanjaro looming over their shamba. Unfortunately the tribal ancestral spirits demonstrated their disapproval of conceit by casting a spell for dwarfism upon Samson. A meagre four foot ten was not conducive to personal power in African society and he had learned to make up for this lack of physical prominence by clowning and teasing, to attract attention.

He furthermore boasted that he, 'had been chosen to cook for Her Majesty Queen Mother' when she visited Kenya. He intimated that he should receive extra pay since he was By Royal Appointment. Jo gave him a steady disbelieving stare and offered him 120 shillings a month. He was soon round with his blanket and his wife Magdelena. She was very tall and slim as a broom stick. They looked like a bat and ball together. We soon discovered that the bat was demure and the other a ball of fire. After Samson's evening of celebration over his new appointment, in the local *pombe* bar, we found him behind the house mercilessly beating Magdelena with a broomstick. Jo's reaction was to snatch the broomstick and beat him with it, plus threatening language. In England these days one can be charged with assault for beating a burglar, never mind a house servant, but in Africa's black and white thinking Christian society the 'an eye for an eye' concept prevailed. This incongruous couple soon settled happily into our servants quarters behind the kitchen.

The word had obviously gone round that we had lots of children and a 'nurse maid' arrived on the door step. She was admirably photogenic, bare from the waist up, young with full breasts and a complex bead necklace. She couldn't speak a word of English, but she obviously thought the master of the house would fancy her. Well... the camera's eye recorded her charms, with snow capped Kilimanjaro in the background.

Before my departure I was advised by the Senior Research Officer that President Julius Nyerere's orders were to concentrate on settling Africans on the land as farmers and no more serving white commercial farmers, as my predecessors had exclusively done.

'And Brian, we are told that the peasants must learn modern methods of food production, in other words, hybrid maize, chemical fertilisers, herbicides and tractors to replace hoes. And they can't wait. That's politics for you. Not sure that it's sound agro-economics.'

My job was to be planning land development schemes for Africans, which was in accord with our ambitions. Bill was anxious to get away on leave and had planned a lengthy motor safari in his *Peugot 303* rugged tank-like car starting with a 250 mile drive down to steamy Tanga on the coast. Everywhere we went people along the roads raised a clenched fist, and smilingly shouted *Uhuru*, meaning Freedom.

From the sisal port of Tanga we returned to climb the winding mountain road into the Usambara Mountains where there was a rest house at an old German Station called Amani, meaning peaceful. This turned out to be a delightfully cool place in temperate rain forest, carpeted with St Paulia or wild African violets. Expatriates frequently gathered there for convivial dinners, as did the Germans before they were cleared out in 1917. The Germans reached Amani by a mountain climbing mono-rail powered by slave labour.

Passing Kilimanjaro on the way back, I spotted something which I have never seen since in my twenty five years in Africa, a distant ghost-like white giraffe. I later learnt that albino giraffe were extremely rare and that there was no record of one in Tanganyika. I snapped it with my pocket camera but did not have a telephoto so that my report has always been treated as a planner's dream.

We passed through Arusha non-stop in Bill's old tank, racing to get to the famous Ngorongoro Crater before dark. Just nearby at Upper Kitete I was to plan a co-operative farm to grow mechanised wheat, with British aid money.

Many years after planning this scheme for producing high altitude wheat on a large scale, Rt. Hon. Barbara Castle, Secretary for Overseas Development, visited this project. She was quoted as saying that she was "greatly impressed with what Africans were capable of" In fact African input was minimised in favour of co-operative share holding, the employment of expert management, and the use of modern combine harvesters. The scheme still operates today.

I had never before been away from my family. The boys, especially Richard, resented my absence; he had always been with me around the farm learning all the skills. They all had so much to tell me when I returned, six dead snakes, two of them cobras; the water furrow was cleared and delivered fresh grapefruit every morning by flotation, several hundred cockroaches roasted for their sins, PWD, meaning Power and Works Department, furniture had been delivered with mosquito nets on all the beds. Jo had found Fati Hali Dali's supermarket in Arusha, where a baby elephant famously broke loose and wrecked the place - to music, in the film Hatari. The boys had been admitted to the very good school in Arusha, where President Nyerere had also sent his son.

Jo told me that she had decided to be firm with Samson and to try giving him orders in Kiswahili. Each morning he came into the bedroom at 6.0 am dawn, in his new white kanzu and red fez, with tea on a tray. He would then receive his instructions for breakfast.

This time the Memsahib sat upright and declared hurriedly but purposefully, 'Samson! *Blekfast! Mayai mbili fly ndani ya dawa ya viatu!*' which means; breakfast - eggs two fried in the medicine of cooking. Off he went obediently to the kitchen, as any Royal Appointed cook should, sensing the importance of the occasion. Jo and the children sat round the dining table awaiting the outcome.

'Funny smell coming from the kitchen!' said Richard, 'Phew! What's he doin Mum? Shall I go and see?'

'No. We must let him do his thing, and correct him later.'

In due course the door swung open and our diminutive cook, heightened by his red fez, emerged grinning like a Cheshire cat. He marched stiffly in and placed the steaming plates before us. He then turned away and doubled up in uncontrollable laughter. I tried to look dignified, my nose turned up over the pungent offering, as I realised that the black eggs had been fried in shoe polish. Samson slunk out to the kitchen in hysterics.

Jo had confused that other morning commodity shoe polish *dawa ya viatu* or medicine for shoes, with medicine for cooking *dawa ya kupika,* medicine to cook. He offered to make up for the disaster by skinning and cooking one of the snakes for supper as a treat.

'Did you accept the offer?' I inquired with a straight face.

'Ah.... I'm not saying,' Jo replied with a slight tilt in her retroussé nose, 'If you want to know what's going on at home you'd better be here.'

In the Common Room that evening I met a Welsh geologist named Huw Jones. He was working in Maasai land south of Moshi and offered me the chance to encounter rhino. There was a long week-end break ahead so I jumped at the chance. The boys were told that they had to prepare for day school on

Monday morning early so it was decided that Caroline could accompany Huw and me.

The following morning Huw was at our door.

'These rhinos are not the friendly babes that you see in Nairobi Park boyo. I've brought the Game Guard just in case of any trouble,' came the sing song Welsh accent.

'How far is it Huw?'

'Oh… about 80 miles from yer. There's no proper road mind. My Land Rover's a bit like riding yer 'orse on the farm really Brean. Bring a cushion if you like.'

We were soon bouncing along a corrugated gravel track, with the Game Guard, cans of petrol, camping gear, and water *debbies*, under the canvass at the rear. The hours grew hotter and hotter with the declining altitude and we were thankful when the gravel road ran out and were told to make camp for the night. There was no need for a tent we were told, just a bed roll each and a ground sheet.

As the cool evening air descended our wet vests began to feel like clammy plastic. We gathered close round the fire and cooked tinned beans from the Indian duka, and then sweet potatoes, in the ashes of the camp fire. As the fire died down the heavens were illuminated with an infinity of stars, it was as though we were in an astrodome, shrouded on all sides with sparkling pin heads of light, miniaturizing us in time and space. Small wonder the 'ancients' attached so much importance to the all encompassing, unpolluted night sky, of outdoor living. In our sleeping bags we felt as though we were floating in the galaxy like inter galactic travellers.

We had expected a silent night in this wild world, but far from it. Strange sounds punctuated our rest.

Caroline sat up suddenly, 'Huw! Huw! Wake up. Can you hear that low grunting-yawing sort of noise? It's quite near!'

'Oh …. don't you worry now Caroline, the lions round here, they don't have any history of man-eating, or woman-eating come to that. Their deep growl carries for miles, they're far away. We'll stoke up the fire and put the game guard on watch if you like.'

The June dawn was cold and we were glad of our tin kettle to brew up before setting off into the trackless scrubby thorn bush. It was a harsh place, hot, waterless, white, only the fiercest of creatures could survive it, oh, and young Maasai warriors of course, with their beloved cattle. Huw had spotted two Maasai floating in the far distant mirage.

'Ah-ha.… I want to have a chat with those two boyos.'

Suddenly we burst out into an open plain, level as a billiard table, white with saline clay. Huw drove very fast, through short dry grass. Treacherous mounds however were a worry, about a foot high and seemingly made of concrete, built by regiments of instinct driven minuscule termites that learned the formula for cement ten million years before we did. Those mounds could have broken our suspension if Huw got lost in one of his funny stories. We drew up alongside the two red blanketed men, and climbed out.

We were relieved to be able to punch our various buttocks back into the shape that nature intended. Huw did not speak Maasai of course, but his manner of gesticulation was so explicit that we all ended up in fits of laughter. Caroline and I were amazed that these warriors could live happily in such a remote place, with no money, after all what would be the use of it with Fati Hali Dali's supermarket 80 miles away and no public transport, not even a bicycle.

'It's a good thing these lads haven't heard of vegetarianism. They look gloriously fit and lean, on blood and milk don't they!' chimed Huw.

The two warriors sang a duet; a love song to their cows. Their high pitched gentle voices carried on a whispering wind, creating a plaintiff, peaceful sound, so much the converse of their harsh environment. Picture the scene, two tall red men leaning on their six foot long spears, on an almost moonscape open plain, their faces painted up, plaited hair and bangles, as though they are expecting a Hollywood film crew to arrive in that desolate place. They were highly ornamented with copper ear rings and beads, and hair daubed in red ochre. Their apparel consisted of loose red blankets with a belt round the waist, and sandals obviously made from old car tyres. Their blankets turned in the breeze to expose all they took a pride in, especially their rounded muscular buttocks. These men of the rainless plains gazed down upon our little stocky black haired man from the rain drenched mountains of Wales with the same amusement as we did at his gesticulating and bouncing around.

Finally we departed after clasping hands and thumbs alternatively a multitude of times as though we had been friends for years. After a while Huw recognized a hill he knew in the distance and headed straight for it.

'Brean, that thicket over there. Have your camera ready boyo. It'll be sudden!'

29

Thorns two inches long screeched along the sides of our vehicle and snatched at our tarpaulin canopy as we forced our way along some faintly visible track. The game guard rolled back the canopy and stood anxiously clasping his loaded rifle with one hand and the rail with the other. I pondered what else could live in such a hell but a rhino! A deep gully suddenly appeared beneath our front wheels and we plunged headlong into it. Somewhat bruised, we landed on four wheels in a sandy bed at the bottom. The gully walls now towered above us and seemed to take a course bending to the right ahead of us, a possible way out perhaps? Huw engaged four wheel drive and churned off in that direction. Suddenly a loud snort distracted his attention so that we failed to make it to the escape route.

'My God, ee's close!' shouted Huw above the engine roar as the two ton grey rhino appeared at the corner. It raised its massive Palaeolithic head in obvious annoyance at being challenged by our grey noisy tin monster. He had been enjoying a blissful damp hole in the sand bed, out of which he'd sprung in a fury shedding sand. He swung his parabolic ears to get a fix upon us and line us up with his mighty horn. It struck me that nothing short of a land mine would stop this aggressive fellow, he was a positive thinking survivor with a family tree seven times longer than mankind. His attitude was obviously that of a ruthless killer.

He trotted confidently towards us, head in the air, nostrils flared, not only about to charge but decidedly in charge. The odds were suddenly in his favour. Now that we were both down on level sandy ground, jousting could begin. The game guard leapt out and ran up the bank, side stepping the tournament, an inherent feature of African behaviour by all accounts. The rhino was now in top gear, we were not.

The gears crashed and we jolted forward.

'Christ we're in low ratio,' I bellowed, 'Hit the red knob. The RED KNOB!'

As a farmer I knew about Land Rovers. We stopped again, I glimpsed the game guard trying to get a line of sight for a shot, but the beast was right under us as his shot whammed out.

'Stupid bugger! He'll ...'

Confidence in our superiority evaporated, as Huw did a u turn and headed the other way. We hung on to the hand rail; I always wondered why the old Land Rovers had them, as he attempted to climb the bank.

'Can't make it. We'll have to back down.'

'Don't be crazy!' Caroline shouted, eyes staring, 'He's standing his ground; right behind us!'

The game guard took fright and fired again. The CRACK echoed loudly, frightening us all out of our wits; except that is for the rhino, to which it was just a gauntlet in the dust. We had backed right on to him and in tossing his great head he drove his horn through one of our rear handles. At that moment the back of the vehicle rocketed upwards, and then fell again with a spine cringing thump.

We were up again, and crashing down amidst a rattle of tools, cans, hurricane lamps, and my head against the roof.

Caroline shouted, 'I can see him. His horn is stuck under the back handle!'

We continued our switch back ride along the gully. Our kidneys were behaving like yo-yos. Then a change of ride, from up and down, to side to side. Huw was still struggling to gain control of the gear box and find the clutch pedal whilst bobbing about like a cork on a bowl of water.

'Bluddy 'ell!' he kept repeating, and then, 'got it!' Off we went, the engine roaring wildly. He had achieved high ratio, but the rear wheels being off the ground all we got was a screaming engine, and a decided tendency to reverse.

CRASH.

Another bullet, a puff of smoke and then… hissing and steam!

'Crazy bugger, he's hit the radiator,' pronounced Huw as the rear wheels touched terra firma and shot us forward.

We did not move far however as the rhino's horn was still wedged firmly under the rear handle. We proceeded, forward-ish, unpredictably, lurching, rising, falling, swaying, and bouncing, with our safari gear in the back responding like a one-man band. Suddenly the rhino horn disconnected and we shot forwards out of the cloud of dust.

Looking out of the side window I saw the monster heading off after the game guard, who had unwisely slid down the bank to catch the departing Land Rover.

'Hey we can't leave the guard,' pleaded Caroline.

Huw said cynically, 'Let him run a bit, silly bugger. We're not going far with this hole in the radiator.'

We didn't. The rhino kept going in the same direction, seemingly having lost sight of us. One thing that the rhino had taught us was that there was water under the sand. We would be able to top up the radiator.

The guard dodged the short sighted rhino by ducking into a gully and praying. The rhino feeling frustrated, no doubt, paused for a pee near the game guard who was subjected to a dowsing like that from a water cannon. The force of it rooted a bush out of the ground.

We waited until dark and cooler air for our engine. We collected some water for topping up the radiator. The bullet hole was high up and we could move slowly in the dark. The commonest commodity in this wilderness was grey clay which we used to good effect; pounded to plasticine with a drop of water it plugged the radiator nicely.

We drove overnight and made it back to Tengeru in time for *mayai mbili fly*. Huw's comical tale about the dancing rhino, related in lyrical Welsh tones with gesticulations, found eavesdropping Samson unable to serve coffee for fits of giggling.

Caroline later wrote a Thank-you card for Huw, with a limerick;

No fear of rhinos he
So a geologist he could be
With death Huw danced
As the rhino pranced
The funniest thing to see.

Chapter Four

Up-sticks Again

Three weeks after our arrival in Tengeru a telegram arrived from the President's Office;

RE WENELA REPATRIATES STOP CONCERNING BRIAN DAWTREY STOP HE MUST TRANSFER TO MBEYA.... etc.

This enigmatic but respectable sounding official heading swept around the research station, as the explanation of the unexpected demise of the Dawtreys from the social rounds. When Jo received the news of our move to the Southern Highlands she was understandably shattered. She clung to me in despair when I broke the news.

I could feel her trembling, 'Oh God, shall we ever find a place to settle? All that work! Now we'll have to repack our twenty crates… can't we lodge a complaint?'

'Who to? We're on our own Jo. I'm not on the Research Staff list; all Dr Van Rensburgh can do is sympathise. The order came from Dar es Salaam, the Director of Development Division; he is to be my technical boss. Apparently President Nyerere has issued a direct order for a Land Planning Officer to organise a resettlement scheme for Wenela Repatriates from the South African gold mines. There isn't enough land in their tribal area for so many men to grow food. Wenela is the name of the mines recruiting agency.'

'How many are there then?'

'About thirty thousand.'

'*Thirty thousand*! My god!'

'Yes. I think we are an innocent spoke in some political wheel. His Excellency has declared Sanctions against South Africa and its apartheid regime. As it turns out he's the only national leader who has acted upon his word, and I suppose the least able to afford it. He has ordered all Tanganyikan nationals to return home. I am told that the UK government has promised Nyerere a grant of funds for resettlement schemes. I have also been told about a gift of £113,000 from the people of Devon and Cornwall for a farm institute. And there's one other little job; they want a plan for a state farm on the top of a mountain called Elton Plateau.'

'All that for little-us to do, good old little-us. How far is this place, Mbeya?'

'Eight hundred miles. We'll have to get a government loan and buy that old Ford Zodiac we looked at in Arusha. There is a Ford Agent in Iringa, Bill says.'

'And how far will that be from Mbeya?'

'Bill says about two hundred and fifty miles.'

'Oh, quite handy then. Don't see what all the panic is actually, they've done without a planning officer for a thousand years now suddenly they need little-us, next week.'

'Believe it or not, they've already allocated us a good house, and a drawing office, and they've even posted African surveyors there. Almost an after-thought letting little-us know!'

'Absolutely! Well, we wouldn't want to be hanging about would we? Samson! He'll be out of a job, I suppose.'

'Why don't we take him with us?'

'And Magdelena, and three children! In the Zodiac? Eight hundred miles! Plenty to push if we break down I suppose.'

'We'll get a roof rack.'

'Oh, of course, why didn't I think of that?'

'I'll get some Jerry cans for petrol, and tyre levers and hot patches for repairing punctures on the way, the roads are really rough. Only gravel and murram.'

'Should be a doddle! What of our twenty crates? A trailer perhaps ....'

'There's no railway to Mbeya, although there's a Railway Hotel there; they must have run out of steam! The Tengeru lorry will take our crates on

Wednesday.'

'Oh…. Wednesday… no slacking eh. Samson! Caroline! You always wanted to travel. We're packing. Tell the boys, no school today.'

It's no coincidence that Jo rhymes with Go, in fact Jo is her nick-name, her real name is Cicely, which though it reflects her radiant beauty and vivacious nature, suggests to her she says, useless frivolity and prefers Jo. She is a first rate manager, a strict disciplinarian, a forthright goer - not to be taken lightly, though underneath she is a caring, loving and sensitive Cicely. Richard is like her, whereas Caroline and seven year old Philip inherit their father's outlook and more phlegmatic dogmatically persevering, uncomplaining nature.

Caroline is going to have to face a severe test of courage and fortitude on the way to Mbeya; and it is all going to happen on her birthday, poor girl. The town called Iringa, in the highlands, has a High School called St Michael's and St George's, and Caroline is to sit the entrance exam on her 13th birthday the 10th June. It's almost a penalty for success that if she passes she becomes a boarder seven hours drive from home, with just a locker for her own private spot. This is the only High School in Tanganyika, she just has to pass! It is for mixed races but is modern and has an all British staff.

Dr Van Rensburgh and his wife accommodated us for our last night and were helpful in advising us how a young family can survive and thrive in this country, and how to find our way to Mbeya. There are no road signs or maps worthy of the name. They are aware of the high value cargo with which I have to face the worst roads in the world. There are not many turnings they say but taking a wrong one can land you up 100 miles out of your way without you knowing it. They advised that it would take us three days driving to Mbeya, with a stop over in Dodoma and Iringa.

Leaving Arusha's green streets and stunning mountain backdrop behind us, we headed south and downwards to the barren Maasai steppe, a dry and deserted landscape, apart for the occasional hutted PWD Road Camp.

The Ford Zodiac was full of power, and we all felt confident of reaching the other side of Tanganyika, sooner or later. Magdelena left their children with grandparents in Moshi. About a hundred miles out we saw cattle and a group of tall red painted young men dressed in their Maasai red blankets. We agreed that they seemed to have confident, happy, masculine aplomb, with their decorative ear rings, bangles and plaited hair. Yet their tallness, those very long spears, their belted short swords, and their redness, were benignly intimidating. Samson was noticeably fidgety as we slowly passed.

35

I was telling the children, in my usual somewhat professorial tones, 'they believe that their deity L'engai granted the Maasai the ownership of all the world's cattle. They don't listen to any arguments by the Bantu tribes. They consider them to be inferior beings, and regularly remove their cattle to their rightful owners. They beg for nothing, unlike the Bantu, and give nothing. And, if we run out of petrol in this place? We'll just have to... acquire a red blanket.'

'Let's stop and say hello,' said Jo, 'pass my camera Caroline.'

'No Bwana!' asserted Samson suddenly, 'They're dangerous men Sir.'

'Okay, let's wave and see if they are Uhuru-happy.'

I pulled up and they obliged with smiles. We climbed out, Jo with her 8 mm wind-up ciné, camera, whilst Samson cringed in the back seat. They were enamoured with our blonde daughter and stood aloof, giggling and discoursing in a strange tongue, not Kiswahili. They were obviously making a visual assessment of Jo's and Caroline's physical attributes. They leaned on their spears, smiling and gazing at us, much as visitors do at the zoo. They were monstrously vain, calm, and arrogant, adorned with ear rings, pendants and necklaces but beautiful in a long limned way with finely cut features and long girlish eye lashes. An attractive anti-dote to the excesses of civilisation.

Jo felt embarrassed producing a camera. They turned away from what they consider to be the evil eye. She replaced it in the car in favour of a word or two. They didn't understand Kiswahili at all. One of them spat in his palm and offered it to me. Maasai consider spit placates evil influence. I did likewise and we grasped hands then thumbs and hands again, as their copper ear rings and bangles rattled gently in the silence. Their hair was braided and smeared with red ochrous clay; they must have had quite long hair! Their fine features, like Somalis, befitting their North African ethnic origins. I have read that they may have been Carthaginians, and their ornaments were of that style.

The Maasai had always successfully defended their grazing rights, and their customs, against all-comers including Europeans, and now TANU Party men. Their rigorous environment has made them uncompromising. A few Maasai have been well educated, but have been drawn back to their freedom, of a kind we know but little, a freedom of unfettered mobility, love, dress, and from any kind of regulation, taxation, or the necessity of money and possessions. Elders rule by committee consensus - a liberal society. The Morani marry and become junior elders at the age of 26 or 27 years old, up until then their life is one of herding, adornment, comradeship and free love. The Morani avoid pregnancies by loving young girls aged 10 to 13 years old, for which the girls are rewarded with bead necklaces.

A betrothed girl is circumcised, in other words has her clitoris removed by elder women, and has her head shaved to signify her elevated status. The Maasai say that if the girls were not circumcised they would become promiscuous and produce babies of uncertain parentage, thus leading to family breakdown and ultimately to weakness in tribal culture and social structure.

The curious thing about our encounter with Maasai was not our good fortune to meet men who are powerfully free, but the feeling that we might be the misfits in this world. We must have looked ridiculous with our mountain of luggage, our machinery, our flimsy clothing, each of us dressed differently as though we didn't know which clan we belonged to, not to mention our obvious discomfort out in the open, which for the Maasai was the perfect place to be. We felt like termites in the baking sunlight. We gladly joined Samson in our escape capsule.

Our mad dash to get to work continued for another fifty miles. We stopped for cool water from our flask. We were amused how much we were beginning to resemble Maasai in our thick coating of red murram dust. We were beginning to feel a part of the scene. There was a small settlement, nourished by travellers; one of the two hotels proclaimed itself the Halfway House between Capetown and Cairo. That was certainly its only merit. Someone told us this was Kondoa.

Further on at Kondoa Irangi we saw spectacular soil erosion, a landscape of naked ravines and banks of yellow and red striation where nothing grew. Where would the world be without that much disdained commodity that all land-life on Earth depends upon, soil? The textbooks say that erosion is caused by the cultivation of steep slopes in high rainfall areas. That authority was up for question in my mind since this place was flat and only rarely does it rain, though when it does it is intense! What triggered this devastation? These were the things that I had to learn about, in this case overgrazing by domestic animals. But there was still a why in this disaster formula for Land Planners.

Dodoma, later to become the seat of government, was a desolate railway town in the dead centre of the country, of historical significance as a staging post in the slave trading days and for Victorian explorers traversing from Bagamoyo and Zanzibar to the lakes region in the west. We could discover nothing to alleviate the boring atmosphere of the place. The hotel did little to contribute to our relaxation, in fact the night proved one of heightened anxiety with swarming mosquitoes and hyenas rattling the rubbish bins outside the door.

Samson declared that he and Magdelena had had a good night sleeping in the car. He said he'd never been this far but he knew this was the land of the Wagogo, an uncivilised tribe not to be trusted at all.

It was a relief to get away, uphill towards Iringa, albeit with stinging hides. After a while, seven year old Philip aroused us from our torpor and made us all laugh with his innocent question, as though he hadn't noticed the joy and travail of the last 6,000 miles, 'Dad? Where we going?

After one puncture on the rocky road and being tossed, broiled in perspiration, peppered with red dust for two encapsulated days, the highland town Iringa was a great relief and to discover the luxurious cuisine of the White Horse Inn, run by a gentle mannered Greek named Sophacles.

Jo slumped into a soft chair, 'Tea please!'

The Inn was a tonic of comfort and welcoming service for weary travellers, who arrived, like us, exhausted, from far off places like Dar es Salaam in the east, Mbeya in the west, Arusha in the north and Mwanza on Lake Victoria in the North West. The bar was packed with the hubbub of news-seeking local residents, mostly British colonial staff and Greek tobacco farmers.

Iringa town is of quaint German origin and was an important outpost of the spreading empire of 1914 Germany. The air is bracing at 5,300 feet altitude, 2,000 feet higher than Snowdon, perfect for the gorgeous floral garden displays everywhere.

'Thank god we weren't posted to Dodoma!' blurted Caroline over her tea cup. Her hair was no longer blonde but auburn, 'I can see why the British built the secondary school here, and at least you can think in the cool.'

Much blood was spilt here by German and African warriors. We decided to delve into Iringa history whilst Caroline was to be sweating over her thirteenth birthday exams, poor girl. I also had to visit the Agriculture Department Office as I had to cover this Province as well as Mbeya Province. I couldn't believe that it was humanly possible.

The following day we arrived at the school, St Michaels and St Georges, since renamed Mkwawa High School. We were agreeably surprised to find the strikingly modern architecture of the school, set between two rocky wooded hills with extensive playing fields and gardens. The British headmaster told us that the school was three years old and a model of multi-racial grammar education with good boarding facilities.

He said, 'Our pupils are 45% African, with a large contingent from the local Greek farming community and a few Asians and British. The British are from farm estates of tea and wattle in the mountains near Njombe. We have achieved very good academic standards equally between all races. In the dormitories we do get problems from time to time between races of adolescents but Mrs Wiltshire, who will be Caroline's house mistress is very good at maintaining a happy atmosphere. She is also very strict about keeping the boys and girls separate after classes.'

We were agreeably surprised to find, after a study of academic results, that standards were significantly above those of our local LEA schools in Norfolk. The pupils put in more hours, rising at 6.0 am with lessons from 8.0 am until 4.45 pm, plus Saturday mornings. We crossed our fingers for Caroline. It was two and a half months since she did any school work, but we knew that she would pull out every stop to get into that school. The boys, who had previously been at the local village school, were quietly awe inspired by the studious atmosphere at this school.

The Provincial Agricultural Officer was Don Muir. He received me with a friendly reticence that slightly chilled the social coffee. I had to accustom myself to being a new type of public servant, not a career Colonial Service permanent and pensionable officer, but an officer serving on contract to Tanganyika Government. Also the new edict that I was to serve African aspiring farmers and not expatriate farmers, who after all fed the nation as well as produced the exportable commodities, caused some dissention bordering upon ridicule amongst some British staff. I was tactfully reminded that new development schemes like the Wenela Repatriates resettlement scheme, would create much extra supervisory and administrative work for them, and might not be popular.

I was aware that it rankled a bit, that I was a muddy-boots farmer and not the traditional Trinidad College of Tropical Agriculture, graduate. The common room fell silent when I explained that it was the British Government that was putting up the money to create farming settlement schemes as a political move against Apartheid. They undoubtedly felt that the colonial curtain was falling about their ears.

Finally, and with a sigh of relief for me, there were invitations all round from the staff to visit them in the evening for sundowners. Jo and I found them a delightful and friendly crowd of people.

The Asian manager of the Ford garage advised me that my tyre was damaged beyond repair. With a spanking new tyre we set off for the Kalenga

Mausoleum to make our acquaintance with the famous African chief named Mkwawa after which the school was to be renamed.

In 1954 the Governor, Sir Edward Twining, retrieved the fabled chief's skull from the Bremen Museum and handed it to the chief's grandson Chief Adam Sapi OBE, who set up the small Uhehe Museum down at Kalenga, the old chief's capital. The remains of the great wall that was blasted to pieces by the German army, enclosed about a square mile of land and a great anthill upon which the chief used to arouse the passions of his followers before doing battle. Mkwawa conquered twenty nine of the surrounding tribes including a singular defeat of the Maasai at one battle, to which battle he had disdainfully sent his daughter to take charge.

He kept the Arab slavers out of his area too, extracting tributes from their caravans passing through, below his elevated fortress. He later refused to sign any treaty with the invading Germans (Bagamoyo 1888), and three years later the Germans sent a column of 1000 troops to 'pacify' him. Mkwawa sent a peace deputation to talk to the Germans, who foolishly fired and killed them all thus triggering outright war. Mkwawa sounded his war trumpets and routed the German column killing 10 Germans, 250 of their Zulu soldiers and capturing 300 rifles and 3 field guns. This incident was at Lugalo 16 miles east of Iringa.

Another three years passed before the Germans tried again, with even stronger forces. They found Kalenga fortified with stone and clay walls twelve feet high and eight miles in circumference. Imagine the effort and organisation required to build such a fortification with bare hands! But for the Germans all they had to do was to huff and puff and blow the wall down, with their artillery. The defendants fought to the last man, but the chief escaped to organise a guerrilla force and later a battle famously known as The Maji-maji Rebellion. Maji means water.

The witchdoctor made a morale boosting potion of maize, sorghum, and water containing the magic element, probably alcohol or hashish, that was said to turn the German bullets to water as they struck Wahehe flesh. Spiritual power is wine to brave men, but German fire-power won the day and only the chief survived, to be hunted down by Von Prince the new German Commander of Iringa. For several years the Germans failed to catch him despite the price on his head of 5000 rupees. He finally killed himself to avoid capture. The Germans cut off his head and sent it to Germany. Such a man did deserve a monument and an educational facility seemed appropriate.

Richard and Philip loved stories of hunting and of battles.

Young Philip remarked, 'Chief Mkwawa must have been a great guy if he could balance five thousand rupees on his head and still escape from the Gerries.'

The mausoleum echoed with irreverent laughter.

The Germans in their typically determined way dragged the heavy guns from the battleship Konisberg all the way up to Iringa. The Iringa cemetery bore witness to past strife with the graves of many German, South African and British soldiers.

Philip had heard about the many Greek farmers in the area and enquired, 'Did they kill any Greeks?'

'Well ....' I guessed, 'no, the Greeks came in after the war.'

Richard was becoming overwhelmed with academics, 'I like a good battle but all this history stuff! We get it at school as well. Bit of a bore really.'

I felt the need at this point to formulate a line of wisdom. 'You remember when we ploughed the old pasture field at Home Farm, how the barley crop came up all poppies next year, like a bloody battle field.'

'Oh yes!'

'Well, history is like that. The seeds from the past are always there, and can affect everything we do today. Knowing what happened might come in useful.'

I was pleased with that analogy.

'When I grow up I shall use herbicides. There'll be no poppies on my farm,' said Richard knowingly. Richard always had an immense ability to grasp essential functional knowledge. Anything academic fell by the wayside; the epitome of a farmer's son.

Jo erupted in laughter, and then cleared her throat and looked away.

The following day, June 11th 1962, we were all in high spirits. Caroline had passed her birthday tests. We couldn't rustle up a birthday cake and we had little to offer her to compensate for our impending separation, but love, admiration, and some small gifts that we had secreted away when we left the farm in March.

The following morning we left Caroline in the kind hands of Mrs Wiltshire. We found the other girls in her dorm to be vivaciously excited Greeks who did not give Caroline a moment to brood over our parting. We said a brief tearful good-bye and departed with a feeling of remorse, for seven or eight hour's drive, depending upon how many punctures, to Mbeya.

We drove down the precipitous escarpment south of the town, crossed the Little Ruaha River and hit the murram road following the Rift Valley floor below the towering mountains to our left for hour after hour, in a cloud of penetrating dust. The terrifying hazard for all of us was trying to overtake a lorry or bus in that cloud of dust, unable to see whether a vehicle was approaching. There were several deadly surprises that such driving conditions had to offer; such as the rock left in the road by a lorry driver having used it to stop his brakeless vehicle sliding backwards when parked for a pee, and precipitous dongos or drifts laid to take flood water across the road, which when met at speed had a big-dipper impact on passengers, car and luggage. Also very tricky were very narrow wooden bridges with eroded access and exit. Driving slowly was not an option over murram road corrugations which shook the car to pieces at slow safe speeds.

About six hours on we came to a large wooden river bridge at Chimala. There was a white face amongst the team of workers there, so we stopped for an exchange of greetings, as one does in remote locations. Although Samson referred to him as Mzungu or European he turned out to be another of those post-colonial commodities an American Peace Corps engineer. He was one of the very first to come to Africa, his name was Rodgers Stewart.

He had an awesome tale to tell, 'One of my labourers working at the end of the bridge was bitten by a snake. I ran to my Land Rover at the other end to grab my snake venom kit but by the time I reached the man he was already dead.'

We enquired, 'What kind of snake was that?' He didn't know, perhaps a mamba.

On the eighth hour out we blissfully hit tarmac and knew that we were close to Mbeya. It was dark and we settled for the Railway Hotel rather than try to find our house. We were shattered. Samson and his wife slept in the car. Jo and I were content to await the morrow to encounter our destiny.

Chapter Five

Mbeya and a Flying Start

'It's the middle of a working week Jo,' I said over our 7.0 am hated paw-paw and lemon at the hotel, 'and after all that trauma of getting here double quick, I bet the office doesn't even know that we're coming!'

'We're mad. I'll bet the Maasai would have a suitable word for our behaviour.'

The open windows of the dining room heralded the sounds and smells so typical of Mbeya, that loud coarse cawing of pied ravens in the tall scented eucalyptus trees. There was no other sound but for the waiters busily clinking spoons and cereal bowls.

By 9.0 am we were at the door of our house in Burton Road, our boxes having miraculously overtaken us somewhere. Africa never ceased to surprise us. Loleza Mountain loomed up behind the house, a pretty bungalow style residence with a front veranda and servant's quarters at the rear. The large lawned garden was bounded by high hedges with beautiful pale mauve blooming jacaranda trees and bright red nandi-flame trees along the drive. It was fabulous. The air was cool and a water furrow ran through the garden for irrigation. The Department of Agriculture had really tried to make us welcome.

Giant carpenter bees drilled noisily in the eaves of the house making holes big enough to accommodate a fountain pen, and when disturbed they zoomed down over us 'like spitfires' said Philip.

Neighbours soon came to assist us; they were not reserved as becomes the English back home. The young doctor and his beautiful Dutch wife were keen to fill us in with one or two points for healthy survival;

43

'The water supply comes from the volcanic mountain streams. It's quite drinkable but contains fine mica and needs to be filtered. The air is full of fine mica dust too, but only in certain weather conditions.'

I had visions of us suffering mica clad sinuses after a few years.

'Do wash your vegetables and fruit Jo. I use potassium permanganate. Just a precaution against amoebic dysentery. There's no cure.'

'How about malaria and bilharzia?'

'We're lucky there, it's too cool, no problem.'

The chat turned to our safari from England and who we were, the nature of our family and the nature of their family, and whether they would like us to send the vegetable man round today. We said yes. He later arrived and turned out to be a handsome boy of about twelve. He told us that he lived in a *peepa* in the market, which is a 45 gallon oil drum. After making some purchases Jo gave him some biscuits, which prompted a promise to come again every Sunday and to bring the Memsa-b an orange.

The small boy was true to his word and came in his Sunday-best clothes. He also brought some friends who all duly received some cake and sat on the veranda steps along with our two boys whilst Jo showed them photographs of England. There was an enlarged picture of my blonde sister Joy in full flow as a career girl, sitting at her office desk speaking on the telephone. The boys were very impressed with her mass of flowing blonde hair. On their return visit's the boys always referred to Joy as 'the queen with the great white head.'

Some very friendly African women came round too. They were most polite little ladies dressed in bright colours with prints of their President displayed on their bottoms. They touched everything that Jo was wearing and giggled. They were fascinated by Jo's white nails. Jo's animated humour set them off clowning and laughing. They responded to Jo by trying to teach her their language so that they could communicate better. They posed for my camera.

Our next visitor arrived on a bicycle, dressed in official messenger blue and red uniform. He handed me a note. It read Mr Brian Dawtrey to report to the Provincial Agricultural Officer, Mr Jonathan Ishengoma, at 2.0 pm. An African! The scene was changing.

The Department of Agriculture was a short walk from our quarters, and part of a cluster of government administrative houses, offices, a court and a hospital, sited, as always, in the upper levels of the town. The Anglican Church nearby, was tastefully designed and built of stone with a back-drop of flowering trees and shrubs. Below the church the road ran downhill through the main shopping street populated by Asian dukas and a cinema, to the market place where lorries daily tipped their loads of oranges and mangoes loose on the pavement. Beyond the market lay the Township where the bulk of the Africans lived. The township was well planned with good services, schools and concrete block houses with small unkempt gardens.

The evenings were quite cold, hence the Forestry Dept., plantations of eucalyptus trees around the town to supply heat energy. Eucalyptus burns green and regenerates quickly after cutting. The colonial forestry enterprise made a huge impact all round the town with hillside pine plantations, providing an assured future for house building materials. If something similar had been done in the Himalayas the current horrendous flooding of the Bangladesh delta might have been avoided.

My interview with the PAO was amicable, and I met several African District Agricultural Officers upon whom I shall depend for local knowledge in the future. They were all well educated and full of enthusiasm for the future. As to the 30,000 Wenela Repatriates proposed settlement scheme, apprehension was again in evidence, and if it hadn't been for the presidential decree the idea of a massive family farming scheme would have been rejected out of hand, because of the huge amount of work envisaged for the agricultural training and advisory staff. I gathered that Johnathan Ishengoma did not want all his staff and resources to be mopped up with one tribe in one place. Apparently these ex-gold miners were all Wanyakusa. Opposition loomed again.

Johnathan had organised other work for me to do. I retreated to my wife for counselling, as ever.

'I don't know Jo, damned if I'm going to be pushed around. I'm not used to having my work organised for me, as you know. He says he's my administrative superior! The days of colonial civil servants obediently sitting around awaiting their MBE's for good behaviour are not my scene.'

'Good for you, you tell 'em Brian. I expect he's just following orders from Dar es Salaam though.'

'My technical boss is in Dar, and there's no working telephone. That's how I like it. I'll tell you something else he said, "if every small farmer takes our advice to use fertilisers, sprays and hybrid seed maize, then the nation's food shortage problems will be solved without new schemes,"'

'That sounds like heaven. It's the old hackneyed question though; why should a slaving farmer borrow money to buy fertiliser and risk following the advice of a well paid advisor who gets his salary whether he's right or wrong.'

'Exactly. I was looking at the Annual Reports. Maize production is falling everywhere.'

'Well Brian you're going to need support from somebody high up; and something else, if you're going off again tomorrow, or this afternoon! This is one peasant that might be missing when you get back. I've had enough packing and unpacking on my own. And what about the boys? We must get them into Mbeya School; they're getting wilder by the day.'

'Yes I'm sorry. We'll stick together and get our new home set up and the boys into school. To hell with the Civil Service and its little tin-gods. I don't even know my survey staff yet.'

I found my surveyors were all ex-primary school leavers with none of the arrogance that one finds with School Certificated graduates. These were young Tanganyikans willing to rough it in the bush and work amongst village communities, often in hazardous situations under canvass, leaving their families behind in town for a month at a time. They would do it in their boundless enthusiasm for building a new nation, much as Jo and I did after the war. Here it was called Uhuru. Of course they needed camping allowances to compensate.

My surveyors all spoke good English and Kiswahili as well as their tribal languages. In accordance with the detribalisation philosophy of Julius Nyerere my surveyors had been posted from all over Tanganyika and of mixed tribes. They had received special training in survey work at Morogoro Land Planning Training Centre. This excellent institution was set up with British aid, and was fundamental to land development planning. They were sent out with a complete set of survey equipment ready to start work. If only there were more such institutions in the Developing World; or in the UK come to that.

Excepting for Alexander Maki, the senior man, the surveyors were young married men, affable, welcoming towards Jo and I and the boys, and respectful in manners. I found their enthusiasm infectious, and I resolved to maintain leadership and logistic support at field level, not from behind a desk! I knew that African departmental heads would look upon men who work in the bush as being of inferior strata of human beings. In the course of time I learned how to overcome African administrative opposition to the provision of camping allowances and Land Rovers for surveyors and that was by mentioning *nyama*. The Swahili for meat, of the wild sort, it works wonders with all Africans.

I was allocated a chunk of Africa approaching the size of England to survey for good land, hence the threat of becoming an itinerant absentee husband and father. The urban area of Mbeya was well mapped, but the next map sheet was blank. I would have to depend upon a compass, some decrepit wartime air-photos and hearsay.

The twelve hour night and day regime of the tropics was destined to give me long evenings by lamp light under canvass so I accumulated a box of old colonial reports and academic books, to swat up the various ologies that I needed to do my job, like geology, ecology, mineralogy, geomorphology, climatology, pedology. What better Open University than the *porini* which is the colloquial term for bush. Squatting and swatting in the porini; that was to be my recreation for a while.

Jo insisted that she wanted to accompany me on safari, at least during the school holidays and over week-ends. We had always done everything together; in fact we had not been apart for even a day since we married at the end of the war. We had always enjoyed each others company to the point of dependence but now Jo would have to face hazards such as snakes, which she greatly feared, bacterial dysentery, malaria, food shortages, and dynamic changes in social and married life. Several marital relationships in Mbeya had succumbed to stress but our cement was of the best and we would find a way to maintain our togetherness philosophy. We had been married for fourteen years of the greatest love making since Adam and Eve, and that counted.

I would soon be off on my own for my first safari; I planned to pack my shorts and long socks, my binoculars, trusty soil auger, books and reports, mosquito net and my Hounsfield government Issue camp bed. I had brought my .22 calibre Browning repeater rifle with telescopic sight, from the farm in Norfolk, with no query by Customs.

In my office a gentleman introduced himself and expressed a wish to join me in my efforts to find fertile land for the Wenela resettlement scheme. I was amazed and gratified; I had found a supporter at last. His name was Bob Silcock, a Regional Agricultural Advisor. Bob was a tall man with the weathered skin of 34 years work in the field of agriculture, yet still listening. I took a liking to him at once, mature, experienced, practical and obviously concerned about land development for the benefit of the indigenous rural people. He demonstrated commitment; he was part of the scene, authoritative and dignified.

'To get the money for your schemes,' Bob told me, 'you'll have to play the game the Ministry way. You could try flavouring your survey reports and plans with some political spice. Draw the attention of the new African

Provincial Commissioner Waziri Juma; he's an educated and enterprising man with his eye on the future.'

'Most of the officers I have met say that villagers are not motivated to change their traditional methods of growing food. What do you think?' I probed.

'Fact is; change demands incentive. Take yourself; I gather that you are a contract aid-worker with no pension; you must have had a good reason for coming. Evaluating human resources is difficult; which is why economists dodge the issue in favour of building hypothetical production models which look good on paper. We're looking at grass-roots incentives here; refugees from a modern world in South Africa who want to make money. They'll adapt.'

Bob told me that he had the authority to utilise the government Piper Apache aircraft for survey work and suggested that we fly over Chunya District, the size of Wales, in search of suitable sites. He told me that the area was pretty much uninhabited.

I thought, flying to work! Wow! I really liked this guy.

Jo greeted a returning jubilant husband that day. Surprise, surprise we had a guest in the house, a young American woman named Marion. Jo introduced her and explained that she was staying overnight on her way to Mbeya air field and home to USA, after living two years in a primitive Wasafwa tribal village. I could hardly believe my ears. She certainly looked the rugged type of woman, tough to the point of being thick skinned, maybe? A busy mind was much in evidence however, and here was a good chance for us to learn something about this highland tribe that is native to the Mbeya volcanic Kipengere Mountains.

'I've really had enough of their primitive minds,' Marion declared, ' though I have to admire their capacity for hard work in the fields. They haven't even learned to speak Kiswahili yet so I've had to learn their language, Kisafwa. Now I want to go home and write it all up.'

We saw the Wasafwa women daily head-loading vegetables down to Mbeya market, quite often walking through our garden; they had no understanding of private property as such. They grew cabbages and European potatoes in their cool volcanic upland soils, to sell to the expatriates for a good price. So we had a lot to thank these uncommunicative women for. They were distinctive in their goat skins with their next generation bouncing in the hard skin on their backs and a staff to help support their huge loads. They must have had necks like tree trunks.

Marion explained that this mountain tribe were hard workers, devoted to food production, in marked contrast to their neighbours the banana eating Wanyakusa of the steaming Lake Malawi shores who had become ambitious money and power minded, people populating government offices and businesses, and as we had learned, recently, working in the gold mines of South Africa.

Marion was impressed, she said, with Wasafwa primitive cultural pride, 'they are a peaceful people who are totally happy with their status in the world. They have a saying to justify their backwardness - he who has, is never without desire. To strengthen their insularity and their genetic purity from their neighbours the Wanyakusa, they perform clitorectomy on their girls. I have tried hard to get to the bottom of some of these cultural practices, believe me, I even married the jumbe, who was the chief before Nyerere deposed all chiefs in the interests of tribal unity, and I adopted their dress, language and routine. But I failed.'

Our mouths dropped open in astonishment at her rashness. Was there no end to the crazy things that Americans would do to further their own interests, in this case to gain academic status? At least the jumbe got something out of it.

Jo ventured tactfully, 'Do you think it was worth it Marion?'

'Frankly, I did not obtain those vital confidences that I needed for my dissertation. Nor did I manage to influence their barbaric practices. I shall be able to get my doctorate though. That will give me security for the future.'

Jo and I later discussed what expatriates do in Africa. Some administrate and provide security; some seek gold, ivory, or business, some collect souls for power and kudos with the almighty; others collect photographs and contribute to the economy; whilst some study human culture and gain academic distinction for themselves.

'Tell us Marion, did you also sacrifice your passion trigger with your marriage to the jumbe?'

'No. I think they thought that I was not that attractive to the opposite sex. One girl told me that I had ugly teeth and men wouldn't look at me. She had her teeth filed to points like a man-eating shark.'

'Do you think you had any influence at all? '

'I tried to get them to attend a government clinic when they were ill, but no hope. They insisted that illness was caused but the evil doings of some person in the village, usually a woman. Then of course they set about poisoning the perpetrator.'

I ventured, 'Their insularity is perhaps as well in a way, when you think that our historical obsession with imposing cultural change on other people has been the cause of most wars.'

There was, I thought, an ominous silence while digesting this observation? On the other hand, one of the first Peace Corps returnees famously declared to President J.F.Kennedy that tradition trumps progress.

Somewhat later we had personal experience with an Msafwa woman. It was at night when we had a knock at the back door. Jo opened it and fell back in shock as she beheld a blood soaked face in the light from the kitchen. She was accompanied by a young man who explained in good English that there had been a home brewed pombe party in the village with everyone sitting round telling stories, as usual.

The young man told us; 'This woman was attracting more male attention than the others, her eyes flashing brightly in the fire-light. She began to move her body sensually as she drank more deeply of the pombe. A man opposite her became aroused by her forwardness. His wife decided that she was having none of it, and an argument started. However she continued her game of attraction and suddenly the wife leapt across the circle, grabbed this woman and bit off her lower lip.'

The villagers had remembered our house from the previous treatment that Jo had administered to their children. The young man called to the bleeding woman's husband who emerged from the darkness and produced the lower lip in the palm of his hand. The bright-eyed woman was no longer so, but tearful and contrite.

We took them to Mbeya hospital where her lip was duly stitched back on. Some weeks later she turned up again at our door, smiling, lip restored and a bag of potatoes in her hand for Jo.

It was dawn on Saturday when we were awakened by a hammering in the garden. I was impatient to see what project the two boys had in hand this time. Wherever ten year old Richard was, there was always a construction or repair project on the go and for that matter that is still the case forty two years later! His number two, Philip, was always along side aiding and abetting. The Africans called him the spanner boy, in the workshop sense.

I wished that they could accompany me in my work, exploring the uncharted regions of Chunya District, but alas, they were now committed to exploring the depths of their ignorance at their new school in Mbeya.

I found Richard doing a conversion; an old bread knife into a sharp simi. This is the Maasai word for their two edged Roman style short-sword, weighted towards the tip to add impetus to the strike. I possessed an original which I found a wonderful tool for slashing long grass. Richard was hell bent upon accompanying me every where, as he had always done back on the farm in Norfolk. He declared that his purpose in making the simi was for clearing the camp site and for killing snakes. Richard's ambitions definitely did not extend to sharpening pencils for filling in exercise books!

I was concerned for my fatherly role-model image.

'Listen you boys, the politicians are asking me to find somewhere for Mbeya unemployed to make *shambas* to grow their own food; not too far from town. I want to look at a possible rice growing area called Iwindi. We could go there tomorrow and explore the area. What do you say? '

I felt that I had a reprieve.

The boys already had their bush hats on at the breakfast table, which fuelled Samson's fits of giggling as the fried eggs disappeared and Swahili phrases were banded to and fro across the table. Marion loved it too and found a sense of humour at last. Jo unfortunately had to stay behind with her guest, whilst the boys and I headed out of town by 8.0 am in the old Ford Zodiac. We followed a track along the low lying rift valley floor. After an hour we found the pathway I'd been told led to the village called Iwindi. The car scraped the ground and bushes lightly for a while before having to abandoning it, leaving the windows open against the burning heat. It was much hotter at these low levels, and we were soaked in perspiration by the time we reached the village.

It was not a village in the English sense but a poor assemblage of badly thatched mud huts, with a few tame pigeons and skeletal dogs skulking in shady corners. I enquired after the headman whilst the village boys gathered round curiously peering at my two boys. As we waited excitement rose, I wondered if these children had not seen a white boy before. Obviously not close up, and with straight blonde hair too. The village boys began to laugh and clown about stupidly. They were forming a circle and prancing round and squealing like American Indians by the time the headman arrived.

The headman drove them off violently with a big stick as though they were rats, and turned to us with the utmost epitome of charm. He made the customary solicitous enquiries about my health, my family, and my cows, and turning to the boys he said, *'Habari ya skuli?'*

Recognising that I was a government officer he introduced the subject of work, commiserating in a way, that made it sound like the plague, he said, *'Poli ya kazi Bwana,'* meaning, sorry about the work Bwana.

I explained my business and we set off in his footsteps to goodness knows where. He seemed pleased with the prospect of more people being brought to Iwindi, presumably to enhance his authority in that desolate place.

The hot air hummed with insects as we waded through the sparse yellow grass, and then tramped uphill to a stony ironscape covered with spiky Commiphora bushes. A head popped up in alarm; huge watery black eyes, twitching prehensile nose and a cute top-not. It charmed us for an instant before the African boys whooping with joy swept after it waving their sticks, pursued by scrawny dogs. This was the diminutive, delightful, duiker antelope, quite the timidest of small creatures. Thankfully neither they nor we set eyes upon the creature again.

Descending down hill again we came to a likely looking damp green area with obvious ground water. The old man understood what I needed very well. There was even a small stream flowing beyond the basin which could be diverted to flood the ground for rice, with the help of my surveyors. It occurred to me that there may be many similar areas on Usangu Plains which had rice potential.

I thanked the headman and turned back. We were about an hour from the car. Suddenly the headman leapt in the air shouting *nyoka*; the first African word that everyone learns. We all sprang back in unison like a swarm of grasshoppers. Our tail of village boys caught up with us, thankfully minus the duiker, only to flee again in panic at the sight of an eight foot long grey snake that hissed defiantly on the bank. The black mamba is greatly feared for its quick acting fatal neurotoxin. How does one know when confronted by that particular species and not a green mamba or some harmless grey snake? The book says that, 'it has a black lining to its throat!'

Like most snakes it only bites when molested or handled badly, the book says. I suggested to my boys that they take a tip from the Africans and avoid grey snakes, period. Richard began a tactical approach, boldly brandishing his new simi, whilst the African boys stood back, in silence. Should I stop him? This was the ultimate challenge to his courage, and the test of the effectiveness of new weapon too. No holding him back now. His transfixed audience stood still and silent. The snake coiled into a strike pose.

'Watch it Richard. It's ready to strike.'

He drew back his arm and launched the simi from a safe distance sending the snake coiling up around the sharp blade.

'Okay, leave your simi. The headman's gone off to look for a forked stick.'

The mamba left the simi and made off at speed. Richard grabbed his simi and went after it and was able to administer a swift Madame Guillotine. Philip was right behind him as ever and grabbed the tail bravely swinging the serpent quickly round his head in triumph. Philip now held the stage, which he loves, and it had a most salutary effect upon the village boys. They followed us back to the village with whispering respect for our two.

'Philip! I just hope that snake is dead.'

He was still swinging it round his head.

'You remember what they say in Norfolk, a snake never dies until the sun goes down.'

On Monday a whole new experience began for me. Bob Silcock and I and the government pilot sat like peas in a pod, flying quite low in the Piper Apache. It was early in the day and so not too bumpy. We could not cover the whole 6000 square miles so we decided to follow the river valleys up and down seeking permanent water and stronger tree growth. We would need water above all else for a farming settlement scheme.

The vast landscape below was virtually uninhabited, neither was there much sign of wildlife, but trees loved the 44 inches of annual rainfall and formed a dense mantle of deciduous forest. So, what made Chunya District an inhospitable wasteland?

Bob said, 'It's a combination of factors Brian firstly tsetse fly. Can't keep cattle and it's a sleeping sickness area. Then there is the free draining nature of the sandy soils, derived from granite, which means the nutrients are leached out. Good for tobacco but needs fertiliser for maize. The locals can grow millet by burning piles of wood for the ash.'

My navigation skills were put to the test as we swept across the landscape at great speed. I managed to ear mark a few locations for ground study. The power at our fingertips was exhilarating; it excited me as much as an unexcitable person can be. In one wide valley near an extinct volcano in the far west we spotted a large inaccessible village. The land looked fertile and there were wild animals near by. We disturbed black and white sable antelope with beautiful long curving horns, and a herd of black 2 ton buffalo. Wild pigs were everywhere and signs of elephant too. Animals knew where to find nutritious browsing. The old volcano had obviously worked a miracle and I made a note to visit.

The local tribes were called Wabungu and Wakimbu. I learned that they were refugees from their powerful Wanyakusa and Wasangu warlike neighbours. They have survived a hostile environment but they have found a trade in honey and beeswax. The British Government had helped them with regular supplies of free maize, but with Independence this had now been banned by the African District Commissioner. He said, 'These Wabungu must work harder and be more self reliant.'

It occurred to me that Wabungu might make resourceful settlers. Bob agreed and suggested Virginia tobacco as a cash crop that could pay for fertiliser and some modern amenities. The pilot told us that he knew of a Rhodesian white who was growing tobacco somewhere in this area. He remembered the name of the place because it was so comic; Lupa Tinga Tinga.

We flew up and down the road until we found it. We could see brick curing barns and children playing in the garden.

'A hell of a place to live, so isolated!' murmured the pilot.

Nearby on the main road we found Kipembawe, pronounced Kipembaaway, settlement with a government rest house, a bus stop, a government clinic, and an Indian duka. Surely the Wabungu tribe here would starve without the Asians.

Bob said, 'It must be a hard iron-age life here. They will probably welcome your scheme.'

Jo was waiting at the airport with her ciné camera for posterity. I told her about tobacco soils. Her anachronistic question later, 'Just what, do YOU know about tobacco farming Brian Dawtrey!'

With a wry smile I replied, 'Don't tell any body, I'm learning, enough to create opportunities, for the experts to advise the farmers. Anyway we're flying down to Broken Hill in Northern Rhodesia tomorrow morning. There is a tobacco research station there, and they have similar soils to Chunya District. So I'm on a fast learning curve now.'

'Hooray!' she exclaimed, flinging her arms around my neck, 'I would really love to fly. How far is it? Are we staying overnight down there?'

'Sorry Jo I did my best to persuade the pilot to carry you but he flatly refused. Said the extra weight may run him out of petrol. It's seven hundred miles each way.'

'Extra weight! You wait til I meet this guy! He'll wish he hadn't asked us for a bed. 700 miles you say, I remember you used to say it was too far to come back to lunch from the bottom field! Excuses! Now I'm really fed up.'

'The other thing is, government planes have no insurance for their passengers.'

The Piper Apache laboured hard on a cool engine to climb out over the Mpororto volcanoes behind Mbeya Airfield and then throttled back to cruise over the border into Northern Rhodesia. We droned on for hour after hour. The country below us was endless unchanging boundless *miombo*, Brachystegia woodland, just like Chunya District. We didn't see any tobacco fields, or farms of any kind come to that, just the striking polka-dot effect of Bemba *chitemene* cultivation.

The Bemba cultivation system is the epitome of organic farming and has sustained the tribe for centuries. Probably Neolithic people in Britain used the same technique; basically fertility is maintained by fallowing the land under natural regeneration after three or four years of cropping with finger millet, sorghum and cassava. The tops of the trees are cut down and piled round the tree trunk for burning. The tree stump is killed by the fire and an opening is made in the canopy to allow solar energy to stimulate the crop. Hence a series of circles is created, with temporary villages destined to move to new areas every ten years or so. This prevents the establishment of modern services such as schools and clinics, since it takes the woodland soils some thirty years to recover their fertility. Wood ash feeds the crop. The modern generation of Bemba have broken out this poverty grid-lock by working in the copper mines of Northern Rhodesia. Chitemene organic cultivation supported a low population well enough and in fact Northern Rhodesia was not crowded at four million people for a country the size of Europe, but the population is now growing fast.

600 miles southwards brought us to the so called State Land. This was where modern farming began, and the reason? State Land provides security of tenure and encourages investment. The transformation in the landscape around Broken Hill later renamed Kabwe, was dramatic. The railway, built in 1910 by the British, runs the length of the State Land strip from the Copperbelt in the North West connecting to Congo, down to Victoria Falls in the south connecting to South Africa. Copper supported by steam power started an era of material wealth for the people, which was most noticeable at the time of our visit.

Once on foot in Broken Hill, we sensed striking differences not visible from the air, not all to the good. Unlike Tanganyika, racial discrimination here reared its ugly head. The black people were queuing along the pavement to reach a hole in the wall of the butchery through which they were allowed to purchase meat without infecting the shop for white people. We were quite appalled, and feared for the future of that country. We were dismayed to find that the shop assistants, and field workers at the research station, were all white, and blacks were kept at the doorways. This was not the Africa we knew.

The research officers thought that our idea of training Africans to grow Virginia tobacco was a huge joke. Never the less the climate, soils and altitude were very similar to Chunya and we remained optimistic that top quality tobacco could be grown in Kipembawe. Whether our ministry top brass in Dar es Salaam would take us any more seriously than the Rhodesians, was a moot point.

On the flight home Bob and I discussed ways and means. We decided to surreptitiously set up trial plots of tobacco at the start of the coming rainy season. We could also experiment with my idea of a small bush pole curing barn using old oil drums for flues. If the barns burnt down they would be costless to replace. This type of curing barn could accommodate one acre of Virginia tobacco per farmer. A few bales of quality African grown tobacco could be *a fait accompli* for ministry sceptics. Bob promised to dig out a Tobacco Officer from somewhere to advise us. I was jubilant.

Bob was born in Africa, and as he put it, 'I'm staying.'

Chapter Six

Matwiga and Wild Dogs

I was now convinced that the golden granite sands of Kipembawe were a find as valuable as the discovery of reef gold in Chunya in 1926, which started the famous 'gold rush' and which also led to the founding of Mbeya town. Admittedly the prospect of finding instantly marketable gold is more exciting than a year's hard graft with the chance of a bale or two of Virginia tobacco. However in 1962 tobacco was a valuable and exportable commodity and could bring prosperity to an impoverished region.

I drew up a formal Project Initiation Proposal for the ministry based upon the concept of settling very large numbers of unemployed Wenela people on individual family farms of fifteen acres of deep soil with water nearby. Each farmer would be expected to grow one acre only of tobacco. The farmers would live in grouped village communities so as to facilitate the provision of modern services. President Julius Nyerere called this idea villageisation, which basically puts a stop to the problem of constantly shifting population.

To get financial support against a stream of resistance from the Department of Agriculture was a daunting prospect. Never the less I was posted to do the job by the Office of the President so I felt there had to be some support somewhere in the political system. The customary edict that civil servants must toe the line and obey their seniors was not built into my psyche; the ministry egg heads were destined to discover that they had a rhinoceros in their camp.

When I discussed this with Jo she again suggested that it was time for me to try and think African.

'In your African sandals, broker a marriage between the local politicians of UNIP (United National Independence Party) and the staff of Mbeya Department of Agriculture. After that you can infuse your financial requirements,' said Jo.

Bob Silcock offered to carry my Project Initiation Proposal to Dar es Salaam by Dakota and present it personally to the key man in the ministry, the Chief Tobacco Officer. I gathered that the CTO was under pressure to increase tobacco exports to raise much needed revenue as quickly as possible. However there was no scheme anywhere for African small scale producers, the nation depended entirely upon its large scale white farmers, prominently Greeks and expatriate Rhodesians who were becoming uncertain of their future. The Kipembawe area was an unknown, added to which risk, was me, a chap who knew nothing about tobacco production. A disciple like Bob was a god-send for such a small cog as me and I was feeling confident of success as I awaited news from him.

Even more pressing was news of Caroline's 250 mile safari by service bus from Iringa. On the 20th July, the old Albion bus ground its tired way into Mbeya bus station. This amazing girl had endured ten sweltering hours of being shaken about in a cocktail of goats, chickens, babies and babbling women. She emerged from the flurry of feathers and dust coated children, as bubbly as champagne. In terms of durability she reminded me of a farm gate post, she could withstand abuse without being toppled. 'She's made of good English oak, this girl.' I later declared over ceremonial tea. The mention of English oak triggered the hackneyed topic of Lassie the Home Farm Labrador.

'Hope Lassie's doing all right. Have you heard anything?' Caroline asked.

Something would have to be done about a replacement.

Bob returned and we invited him round to tea.

'I'm afraid the news is not good,' he began, 'the CTO was unable to sponsor Kipembawe Tobacco Scheme Plan.'

'Ridiculous!' retorted Jo, as I slumped into despondency, 'So what are we doing here? Maybe we're just here for the beer! And that's not up to much.'

Bob elaborated, 'The CTO, I think, felt his nose put out of joint by our provincial initiative, and also he definitely took exception to our soldiering off to Northern Rhodesia to consult their experts instead of him. He finally declared that the Ministry of Agriculture had no programme for tobacco development in Mbeya Province, so no funds have been allocated by the government for any scheme here.'

'Perhaps they'd grant small money for trial plots from a research vote or something?'

Bob explained that he had pressed the CTO very hard for some money for trials and the response was, 'Sorry, I cannot recommend that area for Virginia tobacco.'

He went on to suggest the CTO visited Kipembawe to see for himself that we have the best tobacco land in all Africa.

'Good. When will that be?'

'Well. He asked how long it would take him. I suggested four days, using the Dakota to Mbeya. He looked quite dismayed and said, "Sorry, that's almost a week. I can't justify being out of the office that long when the ministry has no programme for Mbeya Province". I fired my parting shot about this being a project under Presidential Decree and that it would not look too good if the ministry declined to help. I felt this was sure to produce some sign of blood oozing from the stone. It did... he promised to send us a Tobacco Field Officer, for consultations.'

'That's brilliant, Bob, the thin end of the wedge. With that advice I could grow tobacco. That is, if I could find some money. I already have to fight tooth-and-nail for funds to cover my hard working surveyors' camping allowances.

An air of gloom returned. The next day I was on the verge of jacking it all in and being a good civil servant when Bob breezed in at tea time, he likes Jo's scones.

'Brian, you've given me an idea. If you could organise the tobacco trial plots, and show the new local African District Commissioner, then the ministry would feel more committed to follow it up next season. Keep up the survey work and allocate some of your survey labourers to work on the trial plots and I will organise the District Agricultural Officer to supervise and plant up. Then I'll winkle out that Tobacco Field Officer to keep us on the right lines. That will *de facto* commit the Department of Agriculture to budget support for next year. Wheels within wheels you might say.'

'I am amazed at all this obstructionism by HQ, Bob.'

'It's not the CTO you know, it's the system. The civil service is the worst possible medium for development work, and that's what Tanganyika needs just now.'

'The ministry rules don't even allow me to buy tools and fertilisers from my survey vote. I could be in trouble with Jonathan Ishengoma in no time.'

'I'll chip in for odds and ends, out of my pocket; will you do the same, Brian?'

'Uh Oh. Bang goes my new curtains.' said the tea lady.

'I meant out of your beer money of course,' added Bob timorously.

The children had been listening intently and sharing first the gloom and the elation as Bob's final suggestion made practical sense.

'Hooray!' they shouted in unison.

That was that, no going back now. Children have a way of getting their parents bound-in to commitments.

Thirty thousand Wenela Repatriates at fifteen acres each, plus woodland set aside for conservation and village sites came to 500 square miles. Topographical survey and demarcation was going to take a very long time without modern aerial survey photography. My boss Don Chambers at HQ supportively said he'd ask London for any more old wartime RAF air-photos.

It was now the end of July and the children were out of school. Time to set up survey camp and trial plots in my selected area of forest near Kipembawe, the locals called it Matwiga. Jo and I decided that we'd all go together in our car, with the surveyors in the Land Rover. The boys were enormously enthusiastic; this was what being in Africa was all about for them, camping, adventure and perhaps some wildlife. They would not be disappointed.

We arrived at Kipembawe rest house with a 45 gallon drum of petrol and my trusty .22 rifle, our safari box loaded with fresh food from the Mbeya market and the Tilley pressure lamp to relieve the long bush nights. Since the way to a man's heart is through his stomach, Jo brought her diminutive clown Samson Emile. He soon attracted an audience outside the little tin roofed rest house in Kipembawe, even though he did not understand Kibungu. He was prancing around, like a black shadow, pretending to be a crooked match stick man with bent arms and legs. In the evening I managed to eaves-drop on his performance in my surveyors' camp. Peels of laughter drew my attention, he was impersonated me, the person he called the Bwana Pima which in Kiswahili means Master Measurer, wandering in the bush with his notebook and thinking a lot; what Jo calls my absent minded professor mode. His demeanour at table in the morning however, was quite the model of decorum, dressed in his white long kanzu and red fez, the epitome of a good mannered English butler. We began to wonder whether he had been telling the truth about serving the Queen Mother on her Kenya visit.

Kipembawe village sat astride the only murram road going north/south 'from nowhere to nowhere'. Opposite was the Asian duka, which we explored in depth. There was salt, sugar, tea, Coke, tinned condensed milk, tinned sardines, matches, candles, old fashioned one foot long carbolic soap bars, rice, maize meal, pencils and exercise books. These Asians are the bush aristocracy, and treat the Africans with some disdain. Africans appear not to have the Asian ability to plan and organise forward supplies, so essential to running any retail business.

When Jo and I returned from the duka the boys were enjoying playing with the African village boys in the dry sand outside the rest house, able to communicate without a common language. They made catapults out of bicycle tube rubber and wandered off down the stream. Basically the African boys were remarkably good shots and demonstrated to our boys how to aim. They came back with bird feathers in their hair like Indians.

I decided to take the two boys with me to explore the 500 square mile uninhabited survey area called Matwiga. This name means simply the place of giraffe. I carried my compass and my .22 rifle and a flask of water. We saw giraffes in the area from the air but they were incredibly difficult to spot on the ground, standing still among the trees, their cranked necks and long legs being indistinguishable from branches, added to which their blotchy colours matched the brown sandy soils and the dappled sunlight. It would seem that their extraordinary shape and colour was perfectly adapted to the miombo woodland, which is why they look so out of place in the open plains of Amboseli, or Usangu. Any sharp eye scanning the forest would first spot their large shiny black eyes and darling eyelashes.

I found it possible to drive the Land Rover at about 10 mph between the uniformly small miombo woodland trees, though not in a straight line. I suppose we made about four miles before meeting an impassable *mbuga* which is a valley bog. I parked the Land Rover and we set off on foot. A white man alone can get dangerously lost in miombo. Africans do not seem to have this problem! I believe that the rural African can navigate like a bird; he always seems to know the direction of his destination, and in the miombo that is remarkable since there is rarely a vista or a landmark. I told the boys, not to worry, I could follow a compass bearing out and the reverse bearing back, but that we mustn't stray off line.

I was looking for rocky hill that I had seen from the air beyond the stream, which we could climb and look over the area. We must have walked for an hour. There were no complaints from the boys. The air was still and the silence when we stopped for a drink was strange, eerie. Nothing moved, just the dry heat making the grass and fallen leaves crackle under foot.

The low nutrient status of the Matwiga leached sands makes the woodland grass too poor to attract grazing animals. The herds of grazers such as buffalo and elephant are found only in the wide valley mbugas, where nutrients have accumulated to produce nutritious grass. I explained this to the boys and to keep a sharp look out when approaching the next valley. I told them elephant and buffalo are quick and dangerous in places like this where the wild animals only know humans as killers. The boys forgot about their tired legs and we set off again, keeping a sharp look out.

There was not even a song bird to sweeten the tension of the woodland; it seemed to be absolute nothingness, in a way claustrophobic, being completely surrounded by an army of identical tree trunks. We felt that there might be something of evil intent hiding amongst the tangle of branches, a cobra perhaps, or a starving lunatic evicted from the village? This foreboding unmoving silence was suddenly broken by a slight sound. Tedium for the boys suddenly changed to apprehension.

Richard swung round, paused and hissed quietly, 'What's that?'

We paused, nothing. We moved on. Then there was a movement, amongst far off tree trunks, was it those Wabungu ancestral spirits on the move? We stopped and stood straining our audio and visual senses. A whole minute ticked away in balmy silence.

As we approached the hill I began to think of an escape plan. It was like being lost in a maze with no way out, there was an atmosphere of panic. I thought, no wonder Africans hate trees and think of them as the spirit world. If danger arises, I thought, we'll be safer in high ground. I increased my pace towards the rising terrain, the tress grew smaller and the sky appeared, much to our relief.

Richard reacted again, he was very alert now. We stopped and crouching low to the ground peering beneath the distant branches behind us. We realised that we were definitely not alone. My mind was buzzing, any predator would be very hungry in this environment, and an old broken-mouth lioness could be following us? I cocked my repeater rifle and searched through the telescopic sight. There it was a sharp wet nose and black eyes. Not one, many.

'Wild dog!' I declared.

Wild dogs do not come in ones and twos of course. Soon a pack appeared, round parabolic ears erect, fierce hungry eyes fixed upon us.

'They're tracking us!'

I had heard of African hunters being hunted, by wild dogs, and not returning to their village. Their Persil-white tipped fluffy tails were now clearly visible. Their mottled pattern of brown, black, and yellow broke up their doggy outline matching so well the dappled light of the woodland. How many? I thought I could count 16. A formidable prospect considering that they all had only one thought, and 600 teeth to execute it.

'We're in trouble,' murmured Richard, 'they look like wolves to me.'

'I suppose they are an African version of wolves, fearless pack hunters. We'd better scare 'em off with rifle shots. Listen boys. The land is rising towards the hill that way; you can just see some loose rocks, there look. Imagine you are on the school sports field and about to break the100 yards record. Go for it! I'll follow.'

I sat with my back against a tree rifle at the ready, as they came briskly within range. The lead dog had its head down as it sped forward following our scent. I took careful aim at the lead dog's head and squeezed the trigger. The loud crack of my high velocity bullet split the air and the dog's scull. The pack scattered in alarm and lay down panting. I jumped up and ran. By the time I reached the rocks the dogs had regrouped, I could hear them whimpering, heads together as though debating their next move and which should take the lead. We were now crouched amongst some boulders.

A leader seemed to emerge and they all turned towards the hill and came for us slipping through the dry grass like torpedoes, with their ears pinned back and their tails straight out behind. Their posture seemed more threatening than before, a 20 mph mad charge began.

As they drew nearer they leapt into top gear and cleverly split to the right and left in a frenzy of yelping excitement. My rifle was a single shot repeater, not the gattling gun that I could have done with. With the hill to the rear and rocks all round us, it was a death or glory 'Custer's last stand' situation. Our boys clutched a strong stick each and stood close together they weren't going down without fight. Dog after dog of the right group, fell to my high velocity bullets. They hesitated giving me chance to home in on the other group. Two fell wounded struggling with shoulder shots which scared the rest. They had probably never experienced such a savage response from any quarry. There was a yelp from their leader and the attack was suddenly abandoned.

The pack seemed to melt away amongst the tree trunks and I could hear my heart beating in my ears in the silence. Five dogs lay dead and two wounded. I was forced to put them out of their misery. Wild dogs may be on the decline but there was a lot at stake here! I consoled myself with the thought that wild dogs are said to have large litters, as many as 16 each. I looked at my boys, their eyes were staring. Neither spoke. The boys and I now had a better understanding of the African attitude to wildlife protection, that it was just another mad-cap European idea.

After climbing the hill for a view across the ocean canopy of trees with my binoculars, and hoping that one day there would be smoke rising amongst the trees from village fires, and the voices of children at play, I shouldered one dead dog to show 'the folks' that we weren't telling tall stories and set off to find our reverse bearing.

Back at the rest house Samson's eyes lit up at the thought of nyama to be cooked for the family.

'Not this time Samson. Only dogs eat dogs.'

He wasn't quite sure about that joke, but said he'd give the meat to the surveyors.

'Not baked beans again!' complained Caroline.

The next day we sampled miombo honey given to us by the village headman. We had been looking forward to bread and honey tea, English farmhouse style, but it turned out to be so horribly strong that we couldn't eat it. So far Matwiga had produced two foods that we couldn't eat, wild dog meat and miombo honey.

After a few days work with Wabungu workers we managed to establish a tobacco nursery site near the survey camp and a stream. The labourers had cut large bundles of dry grass for making shades for tobacco seedlings. They knew that bush fires would soon destroy all available long grass. Beneath the pile hid a puff adder. It turned out to be a three foot long muscular heavyweight, a really hideous creature with a large flat triangular head and calculating eyes. It hissed throatily, unhinged its one inch long fangs and delivered a large volume of haematoxic poison into the forearm of our capitao, the head labourer, as he lifted the grass bundle under which it lurked. The poison paralysed the muscle and began its flesh rotting process. It was an emergency that the clinic could not cope with, but I now had the opportunity to test my South African anti snake venom kit. I always carried it even though I could not use it upon myself in an emergency, for the reason that I had discovered my allergy to mare's serum with which it was prepared, during the Coventry Blitz. I had suffered shrapnel wounds and the anti-tetanus serum brought me to death's door.

The puff adder has an unpredictable temperament and kills by lying motionless for the unwary foot. It is believed by the Wabungu to be possessed by evil spirits. Everyone in camp was demoralised especially since every traditional precaution had been taken to placate the influence of evil spirits. Every evening the capitao had religiously placed cassava meal in the dish in the little spirit house. The Wabungu belief is that new gardens require the goodwill of their ancestors for good crops. Our freshly cleared trial plots sported a little thatched roofed spirit house, within which a small dish of cassava flour was daily refreshed to feed the spirits. Each morning the dish was empty, positive proof, they said, that our tobacco trials would succeed. I had politely suggested to the capitao that I thought their ancestral spirits had been reincarnated into bush rats. He agreed absolutely.

The capitao survived my injection and the shock of it all, and three weeks later my spiritual powers were widely thought to be superior to that of cassava, which was perhaps a dubious accolade. The capitao came back to work for us eventually albeit with a huge red crater in his arm.

Our eventful safari had to end in order to arrange wages. We left the Land Rover, and Samson, with the surveyors and all squeezed into our Zodiac amongst our luggage. Loaded to the gunnels the springs took a pounding over the 160 miles of murram corrugations but the Ford Zodiac took its medicine well. We arrived in Chunya to find that the petrol pumps had run out and crisis loomed for our run over the hills approaching Mbeya. I mixed our remaining paraffin and meths and poured it into the tank. The car went OK uphill to the peak at 8,000 feet and then spluttered its last gasp.

'That's it chaps we're on fresh air from here on. All out for a push start. Leave the doors open so you can jump back in.'

I stayed behind the wheel and we went well, down the windey stony road. I glanced round to see if I still had all my family - yes. We crawled anxiously over the rises and swept at high speed round some nasty corners hoping there would be no crawling bus coming up. Everyone in the back of the car sang merrily as we swept down hill with Mbeya in view. The whole safari had been a bit of a fingers-crossed affair and now fingers crossed that we'd make it home on fresh air.

It was Saturday. Our week-ends were heralded by the highland pipes echoing round Loleza Mountain behind the house. Our Scottish neighbour, Chief of Police, relaxes with Scottish Aires in the cool early mornings and is a fine performer. It seems somehow pleasantly appropriate for Mbeya. Jo and I were encouraged by the lilting tunes to linger in our bed, emotively contemplating the sporran.

It was now four months since leaving the farm; it could as well have been four years. We had no idea what was going on in the UK, how many people killed on the roads, how bad was the weather, how crime was on the increase and prisons overflowing, which union was on strike this week. We had always thought those things so important, yet now they seemed totally irrelevant. In fact, to be honest, despite the deprivations in Tanganyika, UK seemed to us like a dark cloud, suddenly lifted. We were now becoming infected by the African mental tenor of optimism that tomorrow was bound to be good. Also, unexpectedly, there was an atmosphere of greater freedom than is the case in UK perhaps due to the dearth of Regulations.

Our children were swept along by events beyond their control, and they adapted quickly, however in Richard's case he had been affected by the loss of the daily round of animal husbandry on the farm in Norfolk. He was also divorced now from that closeness to his father because of his safaris. Richard expected that Africa was only a phase that would terminate back on the farm. He seemed predestined to be a livestock farmer, or perhaps a vet. Adding to our current frustrations we had to accept that Richard was unsettled. He had grown from seed sown in Norfolk soil and felt the need for its nourishment. Last term at school he had been showing signs of tension and lassitude. The medical officer, Don Curry, had recommended a course of mild tranquillisers for him.

Philip was too young to be a Norfolk dumpling, whilst Caroline emerged from Midland clays much earlier on and in any case had the teenage yearning for wider visions.

About that time I was due back from paying staff at Kipembawe. The two boys were nestled at the top of the African Ash tree in the driveway watching for signs of my distinctive black and white Zodiac trailing dust coming down the distant Chunya escarpment. There was a yell of pain and Philip giving the alarm.

Jo and Caroline rushed out to find Richard hung up with a small broken branch speared under his tongue. He was duly gathered up and taken to Mbeya hospital where the Don Curry announced that he also had a broken arm.

The shock set him back. Jo, also, was depressed by these events. We felt that we were paying a high price for our adventurous spirit, out of farming and into a bush fire. Furthermore I was deeply distressed that Richard felt that his misfortune was my fault and he would not talk to me about it. I felt that there was an element of truth in all that.

Philip's school report cheered us up, he was doing so badly in the village in Norfolk where they were obsessed with new experimental ideas about constructive play up to seven years instead of learning to read and write. The British headmaster at Mbeya said that he was a year behind his classmates but was catching up fast.

Some good cheer was occasioned by an invitation to a field party. Ken Pugh the Provincial Surveyor, had just published his last official map of Mbeya District, prior to his departure. We were all treated to a sighting of the new map at this riotous outdoor party up on Mbeya hills. Much humorous conjecture was levelled at Ken over the matter of the initials in the margin where the road disappeared, MBA. Was this to be interpreted as Mbeya or as Ken's last burst of sarcasm for More of Bloody Africa. This provoked another chestnut in similar vein amongst departing Brits. Someone had put a notice over the Departure Gate at Dar es Salaam Airport that read Last Man Out, Turn Out The Light. This typically British humour had gone over the heads of Tanganyikan officials who had omitted to remove the notice.

I found Ken's wife a distracting woman. She had no difficulty at all in getting me interested in her dog. Her beguiling nature bore popular fruit in the outcome. I was to collect a black Cocker Spaniel puppy on the morrow. Her name was Sally.

Sally's beautiful ears were more often flying than gracing her bright eyes, as she enthused over games such as bouncing on the beds, leaping in and out of the car, racing round the house and jumping the water furrow, biting Richard's plaster cast, and hunting cockroaches and gekos. In the early mornings her first duty was obviously going to be to chase the Pied Ravens that called raucously in the trees over the house. She was as clever as a monkey and just as mischievous and we had to thank Sally for getting Richard into fits of laughter for much of the day. There would be no more need for tranquillisers.

It was Friday again, October now. The mountains turned black with approaching rains. For the children these last two months had been a glorious round of picnicking and trout fishing up in the mountains, with Sally as partner in crime. There was swimming at Mbeya School, with Sally. Poking round the dukas for Japanese tin toys, with Sally, samosas at the flea-pit cinema, with Sally and a newly acquired half Siamese grey cat called Sox - shortly to become six, was not to Sally's liking however.

Mbeya was now home.

Chapter Seven

High Heels, Whistlers, Crocodiles and a Python

With the children back at school I was spending more and more time walking the Matwiga survey traverses, testing the soils, often ten miles a day. The miombo woodland was quite beautiful now mantled in its glorious spring red and gold colours, like England's autumn. Tsetse flies were as bad as ever, I dreamed nightly about their sharp 'teeth' cutting into my blood vessels to create a bloody pool from which to sup their delectable obsession. It was just the interminable sameness and silence of Matwiga that could be tedious. Coming across an old abandoned village site was an excitement, something different.

Old village sites were more open, the extra sunlight drawing up the Hyperrenia grass to five foot tall and good for thatching. The termite-chewed old tree stumps standing two feet high under the taller grass, were perfect for pranging the sump of the unwary Land Rover driver. There was no vehicle rescue service!

I pondered upon the utter historical isolation of the Wabungu and how hardy they must have been to survive in such an impoverished and tsetse fly ridden place. Their legs were their primary means of survival and communication with the outside world. Hardly surprising that we chair-ridden modern humans suffer so much with arthritis and slipped discs. I have yet to see an Mbungu elder with a limp, unless from snake or lion bite.

Back at home Jo had become a feature of the Mbeya social scene. She told me that the social life, like the weather in October was getting hotter by the day, with rounds of dinner parties, dances at the Golf Club, flea pit cinema and picnics on the hills, golf and ladies coffee mornings.

The expatriate community was a medley of people of very different disciplines and nationalities which made life interesting. They ranged in elevation from the heady rank of Chief of Police, Alistair Cochraine-Dyet and wife Beryl, whom Samson insists on calling 'Bwana Crocodile', to our own still rather pallid, newly arrived VSO, Tim Smith. Tim hitched lifts around the various agricultural projects making himself useful. This versatility is where the Voluntary Service Overseas organisation scores over young African university graduates, who tend to think in terms of a desk job. Tim's UK organisers did not realise that he would need to travel. I would have to get back to them and suggest a motor cycle if he was to be effective during his two years of service.

After a long and tiring drive back from Matwiga, and an exhausting week preparing the tobacco seed bed site in time for the rains, I was yawningly informed that we were 'due at Scottish Dancing in half an hour' and also, 'tomorrow I have arranged a group climb of Mount Loleza, led by you, being the walker of walkers, with a curry lunch back down here afterwards. I thought you'd prefer a climb to standing around with a beer glass in your hand, right? '

'Ah… right.'

'In the evening we are going to Dr Paul Jackson's to dinner. You know the chap with the beautiful Dutch wife?'

'Oh... Yes please, I mean, er… right.'

'By the way you are the new Chairman of the Kindergarten School Governors. You have a charming friendly Secretary named Jean, the Senior Resident Magistrate's wife. Since you have served similarly at the village school in Norfolk your co-option was automatic.'

'Ah… right… I can always pop off to Matwiga for a rest I suppose.'

During tea on the veranda on Sunday we got round to talking about the philosophy of overcoming hurdles. Jo as ever my morale booster, and sharp tactician suggested, 'Don't take this as a criticism Brian but I notice that you try very hard on paper to convince the big men in Dar that you are a professional to be reckoned with, which of course you are. However you are not an academic, like many of them, neither are you an administrator. Your provincial initiatives do nothing for their cudos. But times are changing; there are now African Permanent Secretaries. African ears will listen first to African ears. I suggest you try to socialise more with the black boys.'

'Does that mean I can skip the Scottish dancing?'

'No it does not. That's something we can do together. And it keeps us fit.'

'I'm wasting away with so much exercise!'

'Just consider Nyerere's socialist ideology, "more power to the people". You reckon your philosophy is to create opportunities for rural people to make a better life for themselves. And you can be very persuasive! So less of the technical mumbo-jumbo for Dar. and more local persuasion. There, I've had my say. What do you think?'

'You're talking politics. I'm a farmer, a technician, a *fundi*, not an orator.'

'I'm talking marketing… your plans, and ideas.'

In late October after another spell of traverse walking in Matwiga with my soil auger and tsetse fly swatter I arrived back home with a keen anticipation of doing a school half term excursion with Jo and the boys to unravel the secrets of the little known Lake Rukwa. This vast steaming lake lies in the bottom of the rift valley along the southern edge of Chunya District.

During my absence Jo had experienced a unique coffee morning at the house of her new friend, the silviculturalist's wife Pauline Proctor. Husband John was a brilliant biologist and a mine of information, not only on trees, but on wild mammals and particularly snakes, which he collected during his safaris. I learned from John that to kill a snake, simply throw a petrol-soaked sack over it. We always carried jerry cans of petrol so this was a practical solution. Their house was a veritable museum.

Jo told me that she and the other wives were sitting on the veranda when the shamba boy and the cook came running through the house shouting, *'Nyoka Madam, nyoka kubwa sana!'* Snakes being common talk in this household, Pauline was not alarmed and assumed that either John had arrived home with his usual catch or one of the ubiquitous black harmless varieties had been flushed out by the garden sprinklers. The shamba boy persisted, *'Hapana tembeya Memsa-b!'* meaning, don't walk - well they weren't inclined to.

Pauline rose casually, collected her *panga* sometimes called a cutlass, from behind the door and asked the shamba boy where it was.

The ladies gathered round at the top of the steps full of curiosity, but reeled back in shock, sending the coffee table flying, when they realised the size of the monster guest that had come to join them for coffee. Such a huge python could have easily extracted vengeance on the snake-catcher's wife, for she was a small lady. It was known that African ladies waiting in a bus queue at night had on occasion been swallowed by python.

Pauline ran into the bedroom in great alarm and returned with a shot gun.

The monster was already on the wooden steps when she fired. The impact sent Pauline reeling backwards and the steps to splinter. The python coiled horribly, jaws agape. She fired again, at point blank range, and all was still. The intruder was ceremoniously measured and found to be nineteen feet long and one foot thick.

Jo said, 'We ended the coffee morning drinking brandy and ginger.'

I told the boys about Lake Rukwa, 'It's in Chunya District about 60 miles south of Matwiga. It's big - 120 miles long and 20 miles wide, good for swimming, no bilharzia because it's a soda lake. Teaming with fish, tilapia and tiger, we'll need to get some spinners from the duka.

'Tiger fish, wow. Can we take Sally?'

'Yes. No tsetse fly down there, so we can take Sally.'

'Yippee ... Sally we're going fishing.'

Jo interjected, 'When you are at the duka thinking about this paradise for fishermen and buying spinners, remember to buy some rubber gloves, okay? There'll be no coping with those fierce tiger fish otherwise. And, by the way, don't buy any more Baked Beans, they're too expensive at £4-50 a tin!'

'Okay!' chorused the three males in a hurry to shop for gear.

'It'll be a diet of fish, guinea fowl, *kwali* and more fish,' I added, 'dog and gun will provide.'

'Dad, what did you say kwali was?'

'Kwali are francolin, like partridge except they roost in trees. You can always hear them calling in the evening when they are going to roost, like pheasants do in England in the autumn. When you hear that call you instinctively grab your gun, well you do if you're a hunter like me, or if you're hungry. They're very good eating.'

Once more over the mountains to Chunya, car heavily loaded. As always I tried to interest young reluctant ears in the history of the area we were passing through. I had read an old book about Chunya, a throw-out from the Women's Service League library.

'Sally, if you are a good dog I'll tell you all about the gold rush in 1926, just before I was born. Mbeya was small then like me, only two grass *bandas*, in fact, built of mud and grass. By 1934 Chunya was the Wild West of

Tanganyika, with tin roofed wooden buildings, swinging saloon half doors, dust, and wild mannered men, and women. Why? Did I hear you say? A man named Bill Cummings found a massive gold nugget in them there hills.'

Chunya had petrol for a change so I stopped to fill up. A plump figure in khaki shorts and a thread bare bush shirt with a pocket full of pencils appeared; I guessed it was the District Agricultural Officer Frank Rawe. I introduced myself in accordance with my new philosophy of making myself better known at local level. Frank, a real old-timer, listened patiently to my plan for Kipembawe. I could see in his eyes that he was thinking new broom with fancy ideas.

He said, 'Well best of luck. I've been Africanised, my replacement is a young African graduate DAO named Ramus Lyatuu. Good man they say. He'll be interested. I've been here for thirty years and the new government tells me I'm not qualified for this job. So I'll soon be off.'

A greying bristly rugged jaw protruded below his broad brimmed bush hat, he continued, 'Where to? Well, can't go down south with an African wife can I? I'll get my pension. Have to find a small place with some land in Tanganyika somewhere.'

Jumping back into my car I told Jo, 'He's been Africanised. So many endings in this country.'

'And some beginnings.'

'Look chaps, over there,' I continued, 'that's the old Gold Fields Hotel. During the boom year of 1934, I read that there were over one thousand Europeans here. Today, just the one I've been talking to, Frank Rawe, oh ... and the White Fathers. By the way, I made a note of how much gold was found here that year. Where is it, ah ... 46,058 ounces of alluvial gold from the Saza River and 9,969 ounces of reef gold. Those are the nougats. According to today's gold price that's ... where is it? ... fifteen and a half million pounds ... wow! That works out at fifteen thousand five hundred pounds per person! When you think you can buy a good house in England today for two thousand, or a Rolls Royce.'

Richard was listening after all, he murmured, 'No wonder there was a rush.'

Half an hour later we paused on Baildon's wooden bridge across the Saza River which flows down to the old gold fields in the valley. We surprised a flock of naked teenage girls soaping their shiny mahogany bodies. They coyly slithered under the water giggling, and waving.

The milometer now read one hundred miles. Suddenly the rolling woodland fell away and beneath us spread shining water, as far as the eye could see. Every time we did this trip our heartbeats jumped for joy when we reached the escarpment running down to Lake Rukwa. This remote captivating landscape must be one of the undiscovered jewels of Africa. Below was a wood and thatch rustic hotel nestling at the foot of the escarpment known as The Outspan, so named by the Bousfields who constructed it and lived nearby. The day to day management was in the hands of the elderly Christina and Philip Nel, famous ex. Chunya gold miners, with many a tale to tell.

The boys sensed something special about the Outspan and immediately begged to extend our visit from a week-end to a week. I conceded that I could travel up to Matwiga and back. So a week it was. The tranquillity of gently lapping water along the shore, the echoing call of fish eagles, the chatter of expectant monkeys near the hotel, and the pull of semi naked indulgence in the warm water, captivated Jo and the boys. I felt I had got it right at last.

Within minutes of our arrival, it was unanimously declared to be heaven. Our clothes were stowed away and not seen again that holiday. How we wished that Caroline could have been with us, but we would bring her here next holiday, we unanimously agreed.

I found an old report on the dusty hotel shelf by Swinnerton. He recorded Rukwa evaporation rate to be four million tons of water a day! Small wonder it felt a bit Turkish- bathish. The skimmed-milk like water was warmer than body temperature and certainly appealed to aspirant nude swimmers like me, for moonlight nights. None of the other water babies would acquiesce to a hippo-happy bath with me at midnight, not even Jo, on account of the other inhabitants there-in with the same idea; monitor lizards four feet long, hippos and tiger fish both with barbarous teeth.

I attempted fruitlessly to persuade Jo, 'Hippo and human can pass by amongst the floating cabbages in the moonlight, each in pursuit of their particular passion. For me it's the warm water caress. For hippo it's the side-salad of the hotel lawn. I'm sure we wouldn't be bothered.'

Jo winced, 'I don't fancy going out there to be nibbled.'

I photographed Christina Nell standing proudly in charge of her establishment. She proceeded to relate how life was in Chunya in her youth. She ran a boarding house for lame dogs and she pegged her own gold mining claim in 1933 at a place called Mawaga.

She said that, 'Women walked the muddy streets in high heels, both black women and white women, each claiming their own pitch for gold digging and climbing in and out of the Rollers of their lucky digger men friends. The Lupa Goldfield had its own newspaper too,' she continued, 'The Lupa Herald. The editor was George Leighton. Over at John Mac Fie's Bottle Store, George was his best customer, until he got his own still. "George's fire-water" was strong enough to anaesthetise an elephant. The diggers had a riotous time. They left nothing behind, but a ghost town.'

The Outspan Hotel was basically a rustic shelter with English pub comforts, a kitchen, and the bar looking out over the lake to catch any breeze. Three small bandas stretched out across the lawn facing the water with mosquito screen doors. Welcome shade was provided by the high escarpment looming vertically behind the bandas and the massive Baobab tree at the end of the lawn. This giant monocotyledon sat tulip bulb-like with sprouting short branches at its top covered in purple bougainvillaea, conveying an air of permanence to the place. The local fishermen said that it was there when Christ walked the earth; I have reason the believe that.

Our friends from Mbeya, Jean and Eric, arrived with their two children aged ten and eight, thus swelling the mischievous potential. Tiger fishing was a bite-a-minute sport for the four children, but hooking them was a challenge because of their steel mouths.

Another guest named Harry arrived from Tukuyu where he was the Resident Magistrate. He was a mature age single man, but very definitely married to his classic Purdy shot gun. Eric brought his shot gun also, hence, the bar comment that with two magistrates and three guns the ducks were in for some capital punishment at dawn.

We were aroused at dawn by the operatic echo of yodelling fish eagles. We were thrilled to see vast flocks of quixotic whistling white faced tree ducks flying low over the water, in seeming thousands. 'Whistlers' have abandoned their evolutionary custom of sleeping on water in favour of roosting in trees because of crocodiles.

We set off at a fast pace towards the mud flats confident that we would have no trouble in shooting a full bag, perhaps with one shot? However after hours of toil and miles of trudging in soggy 'tackies', or trainers as they are now called, we recorded, zilch. A thousand ducks on the mud flats may look easy meat to the uninitiated but they are unapproachable, like zebras flouncing their stripes out on the open plain, safe as houses.

Eric had the answer;

'We need a canoe, a dug-out, it's the only way. We can sneak up on 'em, disguised as fishermen. Tomorrow's a holiday; we'll have duck for lunch.'

The echoing opera awoke us again, but this time there were additional voices coming across the tranquil water. Part-singing fishermen, parted the morning mists in their canoes. Mr Nel told us that they were superstitious and sing to drive away the evil spirits.

'There are real dangers of course, sudden storms are deadly, and many capsize and are killed by hippos. Two Game Guards were killed last year out on the lake. A male hippo crunched their canoe. Hippos are more dangerous than crocs when you're out on the water. Crocs attack on the shore.'

Our first attempt at attack by dug-out was cine-filmed for posterity by Jo. The stars of the movie were Brian, Eric and Harry, intrepid hunters regaled in broad brimmed felt hats, Mexican style cartridge belts, safari shirts with pockets and lapels for accoutrements, shorts and tackies for wading. The hunters deftly wedged themselves in the bottom of the dug-out in line astern and guns held aloft settling down to hold their weapons vertically between knobbly knees as the hired fisherman pushed off and leapt aboard. Ahead lay the unexplored expanse of twinkling sea, crocodiles, hippos and hopefully ducks. The helmsman with paddle drawn did not sit, like the others, in the bottom of the craft but straddled the craft at the stern.

We saw wives and children waving sadly from the shore, as Viking wives must have done to their warriors bound for Scotland. Suddenly our cylindrical craft developed a list to starboard which grew increasingly impossible to rectify. Alarm turned to hilarity as the canoe rolled over and deposited the hunters, hats down, in the mud. The spirits of the lake were kindly disposed however, giving the intrepids a salutary soak in only three feet of warm water, the tiger fish having fled for their lives and the hippos happy to grunt and snort amongst themselves as they debated the foolhardiness of the performers.

We were able to wriggle out under water and revert to a more dignified bi-pedal posture followed by serious emptying of lake from barrels, and hasty drying with hankies. A further attempt was successful, this time at the squat.

During our absence at the breakfast table battle ensued between resourceful children and crafty vervet monkeys with sharp teeth and coil springs in their under-carriages. The result was a 50/50 compromise, the bananas for the monkeys and the corn flakes for the humans.

The plan for the day was alternating tiger fishing to exhaustion with total immersion. Young Philip loved to savour the power of dangerous animals. He enquired of Mr Nel whether the crocodiles were dangerous.

He replied, 'When I was gold mining the lake was teeming with them, but white hunters, lamping at night, have killed almost all of them now. Just the odd one or two. They live on fish and the population of Tilapia has now exploded. They are thick in the water. You can't see them because of the milky colour but you can feel them nibbling up and down your legs looking for algae, which they live on. You can't catch them on a hook but run a long net out and by the time you reach the end the net will be loaded with delicious fish ready to haul back in again. That's what the Africans do in their canoes. They sun dry them into kippers and sell them to the truckers who travel to the Northern Rhodesian Copperbelt. It's the new gold for the Africans hereabouts.'

Whilst I was away at Matwiga, Jo took the children up to a wonderful whitewashed villa style house on the cliff overlooking the lake and above the worst of the mosquitoes. The place was called Msisikaunga, the home of the Bousfield family. Father and son had made a living as White Hunters, and especially by killing crocodiles for the skin trade before and after the war.

There were five children, plus our two making a very happy band playing together, and swimming in the pool below a cool waterfall further along the escarpment. Msiskaunga was without doubt the paradise of paradises, though of course utterly isolated. Mrs Bousfield taught the children herself on an overseas tutorial course. Their classroom was the open air, shaded by borassus palms, overlooking 2,000 square miles of lake, in the musical silence of the wild, in other words yacking hornbills; yodelling sea eagles; the ubiquitous monkey chatter and the brushed-cymbal like sound of rustling borassus palms.

Of course the Bousefield children had never known anything else, but today they must surely look back and pine for such a place, for it is no more, as indeed for our own adult children today who still seek the warm joy and tranquillity of Rukwa in Spain, Portugal and Florida, but of course such is the stuff of dreams.

Jo took me there later.

Mrs Bousfield said somewhat solemnly, 'It's on the market if you're interested. We're emigrating to Bechuanaland where there is more game. Of course there is no market for this place now with Independence. It will just fall into ruin. Such a tragedy.'

She gave us a white hunter brochure from years ago. It illustrated how they used to make a living and describes the lake habitat and the history of the lake very well; a unique document. The Bousfields knew what they were doing when they sited their house there, approachable from only one side along a narrow track below the escarpment, up above the ravages of foraging hippos and mosquitoes, below the tsetse woodland, a jewel caressed by gentle breezes from a world of water. Instead of Hi-fi and TV they had the music of 400 species of birds. I feel that it is worth recording for posterity a summary of the content of the Bousfields' brochure, a forgotten history in a wild setting.

Nota Bene: African fishermen repeatedly told me that there were no crocodiles in the lake now. This pleases them because not only do the crocs eat women and children, but also tilapia upon which they depend for a living. Hence the fishing industry is booming and the fishermen are looking for outboard motors. I watched fishermen paying out their nets, suspended by very buoyant wooden floats, for twenty yards. At the end of the run they circled round once only, banging their dug-outs with their paddles to startle the Tilapia, and then hauled in the net. Despite the short time lapse, the net was full of fat fish.

I can vouch for the survival of the Puku. It is very difficult to reach the plains on the south side and the west of the lake where game abounds in a Controlled Hunting Area, but I did reach there years later and took a photo of puku.

As a natural phenomenon, the little known Rukwa Rift Valley is on a par with the famous Serengeti, that is if you exchange the grassy plains of Serengeti for twenty miles of soda lake. Rukwa is not a National Park of course, there are no tourists, and African tribal interests prevail. The gold diggers have gone the Red Locust Control people have moved out and the White Hunters too. Homo habilis would have thrived here just as Homo sapiens do today, but new technology and market forces will surely bring pressure sooner or later.

African porters carried Dr Livingstone's body across the centre of Lake Rukwa on their way to Zanzibar, in 1873, as reported by his servants Chuma and Susi. Therefore the lake was dry in 1873, as it was in 1948 and again in 1954 and 1955, when lorries were driven across it by Red Locust Control, who also recorded lake levels. A picture of fluctuations emerges from these records, therefore, which relates to the rainfall pattern over the 40,000 square miles of catchment-area of Chunya District. In 1964 the lake level was the highest in living memory and probably the highest in 2000 years. This is born out by the fact that great old Baobab tree fell over at the Outspan Hotel. Baobabs cannot stand in water. Kew gardens asked me for my photograph of this rare event.

It looks as though we were witnessing an untypical high rainfall pattern in East Africa at that time. From the graph of reported lake levels there is a pattern of sevens and a twenty five year cycle. I was able to predict correctly from this cycle, a continental drought beginning in 1979, and again in 1988 with flooding again in 1995 and drought in 2002.

Chapter Eight

Simba and Plenty Peace Corpers

After lunch I raced 160 miles to my tobacco trial plots. The site was called Lindi. I needed to make a report to the Rural Development Committee of which I was now a member in line with my philosophy of engendering local political enthusiasm. I reached my surveyors camp, known as Mazimbo, after dark, and spent the evening chatting with four of my surveyors, round the camp fire to the accompaniment of the rainy season chirping of frogs along the freshly invigorated Mkowiji stream.

My surveyor's names were Thomas Athumani, an Mbulu from the north near Ngorongoro Crater, a slim good looking young man in a dapper way, with a sharp moustache, Thomas Ngunwa, Valentino Sebastiani, another good looking fellow as his name implies, with fairer skin and more coastal Arabic features. He was perhaps a little too suave in manner for good relations in camp. Valentino was the cleverest surveyor. Michael Zuberi was a modern refined young man educated at a mission school and of a more western cultural outlook.

We sorted out the usual weekly shauris after which everyone was happy and spirits not dampened by the heavy rain that steamed off the bell tents.

Thomas had pegged out the trial plots and entertained Mr Dreisson the Tobacco Field Officer secured by Bob Silcock as promised to us by the CTO. I was informed that he was an affable Dane. So, excellent news. Old Frank Rawe the retiring DAO Chunya, had been up here also, another success. The tobacco crop was planted up and growing well on the ridges by the stream at Lindi.

Valentino was in charge of setting out the soil survey and topographical survey grid in Matwiga, which was at times hard work, cutting lines through woodland and taking thousands of level readings. Some of the younger surveyors had produced comic topographical maps on their plane tables. This was called interpolation, of level readings into contour lines. Their maps showed horrifying embankments and ditches like some archaic fortress in an otherwise level area. I spent many fruitless but toilsome hours walking for miles trying to locate these bits of archaeology, which Valentino seemed to find amusing rather than regrettable. Of course they did not exist. If Valentino had been familiar with Shakespeare he might have labelled their maps a Comedy of Errors. Oh for some decent aerial photography.

The following day in camp I was surprised at the early return from Matwiga of Thomas Athumani. He came into camp driving madly, leapt out of the Land Rover looking distraught, and gabbled excitedly in his native Kimbulu tongue which no-one could understand.

'Speak English please; we don't know what you're talking about.'

He declared that he couldn't carry on the work, 'It is too dangerous!'

'Dangerous?' I quizzed, 'you mean snakes or what?'

'Simba Bwana, lions. I was looking through my dumpy level at the far measuring staff and simba walked into my scope and looked me straight in the eye, as close as you and me. It was *me* he was looking for.'

'I've never heard of lions round here. There's no food for them in this miombo, you know that.'

'There is now Bwana, it is me! Truly! It was a lion Bwana, ask the staffman. Where is he ... *Lettuce! Njoo. Uona simba, ndio?* You saw lion, yes?'

'Ndio naona.'

'He just wants a transfer,' was a murmured comment by Augustine the chainman, in Kiswahili.

Augustine got his just deserts for that sarcasm, it was in the small hours that night. I was aroused from my sleeping bag by pandemonium breaking out in the camp. I scrambled out of my mosquito net in great alarm grabbing my .22 rifle en route to an illuminated scene. There in the beam of the Land Rover headlights was a lioness in the entrance to the bell tent two up from mine, tugging violently at something jammed in the canvass. The men were banging their four gallon tin debbies and shouting, apparently frightening away the rest of the pride, but this one was determined to drag Augustine from his camp bed, to which he clung desperately. Obviously the lion had its teeth sunk deep into the poor screaming man's shoulder, probably crunching the bones as well.

The struggle was now well flood lit and I took steady aim. I had high velocity hollow-nosed bullets, not legal for lion hunters but adequate for this occasion. I went for the shoulder to cripple the beast. The animal roared with pain, released the chainman and turned on me. Its charge ended in a gambol at my feet knocking me flying. I fell against the Land Rover door which gave me my only chance of escape. The cab was crowded!

It had been a close shave for me as well as the chainman. Then all was silent. We strained our ears; only the thumping of hearts and the Mkowiji stream splashing its way through the reeds. We drove around looking for the wounded lioness put could find no trace of her. Back in camp Augustine was sitting up dazed, shocked and bleeding. Thirty seconds had seemed a lifetime; it nearly was for the chainman. We gathered the remains of our courage and went to his rescue, half pensive of another attack out of the darkness. Pressure lamps were lit and we loaded the casualty onto a mattress and wrapped him in blankets in the back of the Land Rover.

'Okera! Drive fast enough to ride over the murram corrugations; otherwise the vibration will surely kill him. The others will be supporting him in the back, don't worry. Get the medical assistant out of his bed at the Kipembawe clinic. When his wounds have been bandaged bring him back here and we'll take him to Mbeya hospital tomorrow in the daylight.'

I was most apprehensive about the 160 mile drive to Mbeya.

Augustine survived it all, in fact I made him an Office Orderly on regular pay, and he became a valuable ally at HQ in championing the cause of the men who toiled in the bush, for the nation and who needed priority for their camping allowances and transport. He also apologised to Thomas for his sarcasm, feeling sure that was why he was punished by the lion.

My married surveyors seemed not to mind seeing their wives once a month, though doubtless they enjoyed the village girls, but not for me I always made haste to get back to Mbeya.

For a white man trying to get political and financial support from an African RDC, despite enjoying gracious manners, was like being in a maze of hidden-culture motivations. I needed to cultivate a kind of deviousness, propounding African ideals and suggesting that their idea of supporting a tobacco scheme at Kipembawe for the Wanyakusa would need positive action by them to please Mwalimo, meaning teacher, as the President has designated himself.

That month's African RDC news told of 200 African teachers dismissed from this region's schools! Why? No money for salaries. Some teachers had agreed to carry on without pay for now in the true spirit of Uhuru. Someone suggested accepting Yugoslavian offers of aid for Kipembawe in the form of bulldozers to clear the bush. This was going to be hard to resist but filled me with apprehension because the Yugoslavs haven't a clue about conserving the thin topsoil and they could leave behind a sandy erosion-prone desert. Salvation cometh in the form of 200 Peace Corps teachers. It occurred to me that Tanganyika could end up with more Americans than ever there were British under colonial rule. The popular phrase that African politicians frequently used for Americans was 'neo-colonialists'. I never could understand it at the time, but retrospectively it makes sense.

HQ ordered me to attend a planning conference in Morogoro. With Jean and Eric looking after our two boys, Jo and I took the murram road to Iringa with two friends as passengers. They were Peace Corpers as the Africans called them, and had become good friends. They were the first Peace Corp ever to come out from USA, the spearhead. They were Rodgers Stewart a civil engineer, and Griff of Forestry. They were diligent workers and good company.

We dropped them off in Iringa after an overnight stay at the luxurious White Horse Inn and continued our downhill drive through the spectacular mountain gorges of the Great Ruaha River, ever lower and hotter until we reached the coastal plain and the wildlife paradise of Mikumi Game Park. We met vast buffalo herds crossing the road, thousands of tons of prime beef. Why United Nations advisors wanted to introduce cattle schemes with all the problems of tsetse fly, water supply, fencing, dry season grazing etc. I could not imagine. I was told that more buffalo got killed by passing traffic and trains than by poachers, which was encouraging.

At Morogoro we booked in late at the planters-style Acropol Hotel, just twelve hours driving time from Mbeya. I had to attend a Land Planning Conference at the British-run Survey Training Centre. We awoke next day to find ourselves overlooking the beautiful Uluguru Mountains that formed a backdrop to interminably boring sisal estates, spreading in every direction on the red soil plain. The bold spiky plants were laid out in regimental lines and squares of nothing else, a veritable desert of sisal.

The main roads were lined with kapok trees, which in the dry season created a fluffy comfy bed at the road side for migrants seeking the gruelling task work of cutting sisal spears. The town was contrastingly pretty, the streets lined with the red flowering flamboyant trees and with floriferous expatriate tended gardens.

The conference proved to be a most tedious formality with lectures by died in the wool permanent and pensionables. Their subject was, what we should be doing and how, which, I have to say proved to have strikingly meagre resemblance to the actuality of life at the grass roots in that new-born nation. Having been thoroughly grilled in the manner of changing our evil ways to a more conformist behaviour, we were terminally advised that there would be no funds whatsoever anyway, which rather made the conference look a total waste of time.

The one bright spot came just as I was terminally nodding off, when my name suddenly flashed into my subconscious!

'Elton Plateau is the only project that has any prospect of funding. The United Nations Development Programme have taken the bait and will consider funding a major scheme based upon wheat growing and wool sheep production, subject that is, to a satisfactory land-use plan from the Planning Officer Brian Dawtrey.'

Huh? Pardon? What was that?

Back at The Acropol we enjoyed some jolly evenings with Agrics we'd never met before. John English of HQ was a man after my own heart, determined to get something done. He reckoned that he might be able to organise £6,000 worth of US World Food Programme maize and dried milk for Kipembawe Scheme. Wonderful news! However there was a problem of transporting it so far up-country from Dar es Salaam port. We would have to continue peddling our wares to overseas aiders of whatever ilk. I now had a second ally John English.

Our Acropol evenings were a mixture of interesting self-reliant personalities, spiced by a shot of Jo sauce. Two gullible naive Peace Corps girls and a fountain of Kilimanjaro lager provided additional comic canon fodder. The effect was as good as amateur theatre. We learned inter-alia that thirty three Peace Corps girls had passed through the hotel this week, on their way up-country. We learned that each was armed with a cabin trunk full of paper back books about US history, social and political theory, family health and hamburger philosophy, for distribution to *'the watu'* , in other words the gullible common folk, or so they thought. They were also armed with jumbo sized cartons of pills for survival in darkest Africa.

The girls favourite conversation catalyst with strangers was, 'Do have a cookie.'

Cookies also served as a parrying weapon for any over-amorous Agric who would get the packet thrust in his face with a sharp rebuff, 'Here have a cookie!'

Two such do-gooder girls had us all malevolently labelled as evil colonialists in need of re-education. Hitching a lift with Jo and I was however seen as an opportunity to fulfil their mission, not as scrounging. During the journey up to Iringa we were indoctrinated with the whole Peace Corps philosophy, punctuated with cookies. The girls were trained in human relationships in other words to, 'identify with the natives, join their society, experience their hardships and problems, and teach them the three Rs; Rights, Responsibilities, and Rehabilitation - into democratic society', American style.

I told the girls that we had heard that, some Peace Corps girls were going about topless in the villages, wearing dirty *kangas*, rarely bathing, and carrying pots and baskets on their heads, even eating *posho*, which is African mealie-meal, and beans, with their fingers, from communal pots, as well as being easy bait for boorish African youths. The African response to all this was of course, 'These Peace Corpers are no better than Africans, what can we learn from them?'

I asked the girls, 'Why do you think that Africans will show respect to primitive behaviour?'

After a pause one said, 'Guess we have to do whatever it takes.'

Which, it seemed to me, did not actually mean anything at all.

In the Ruaha Gorge a Mercedes car, driven by a stout Asian, overtook us and showered us with stones, smashing our windscreen. He did not stop. We then faced 100 miles of dust and perhaps a rainstorm. We soon learned that the trick was to close all the car windows and vents thus creating an air pocket in the car that rebuffed most of the dust. We stopped periodically in the gorges to admire the roaring river and to wash off our red dust masquerade, and consume a cookie.

We dropped the two sloppy Peace Corpers in Iringa and rushed down to St Michael's and St George's School to collect Caroline. She was already packed ready to jump into our Ford Zodiac, even though there was a few days term left. We had to explain that we could not leave for home immediately because of the need for a new windscreen to be flown up from Dar es Salaam. To make amends we organised an evening get-together with our hosts the Mansfields, plus Peace Corp friends Rodgers and Griff. Rodgers was very good looking fellow with a charming manner, just right for a blonde teenage girl to test the impact of her newfound physical attributes. Furthermore he played the guitar.

Caroline, age thirteen, was captivated by Rodgers. After supper she boasted that she did the twist on stage in front of the whole school and it was a big hit.

Rodgers peddled the hackneyed line, 'Caroline, you've got the looks to be a big hit on Broadway one day. Do you know where that is, Caroline?'

'In America somewhere,' she replied somewhat nonchalantly.

'Any idea where America is?' enquired Griff with the dumb-blonde concept in mind.

'Oh yes,' she said vaguely, consumed with other thoughts on the matter of attracting Rodgers, 'We do American history. Christopher Columbus and all that ... he invented America.'

Smiles all round as she blushingly realised her slip of the tongue, 'I mean discovered.'

Griff chipped in again, 'Guess the folks back home in Alabama will be chuffed to know what you English girls learn in Tanganyika schools.'

Caroline retaliated, 'I'll bet you didn't even learn about Africa at your school in Alabama. I'll bet you didn't even know where Africa was until you landed at Dar es Salaam airport, right!'

She was right.

Poor old Caroline. Swooning over Rodgers, we had to drop her back at school for the night. When we left her she was chewing gum.

Bob Mansfield and his wife, with whom we were staying, told us rattling good tales about their eventful lives. They were the perfect marital union, they did everything together. They told us about their recent robbery. They were sitting up in bed drinking early morning tea, as one does in Africa, with the crisp Iringa air drifting in through the open windows. Unknown to us, a thief was lurking just outside. He must have puffed a fine powder into the breeze which drifted across to our bed. We both went into a kind of trance state, and actually watched the thief climb in through the window and collect all the new clothes that we brought back with us from leave in England, and some other items. We just sat there watching and couldn't move a muscle. The police, as is their way, went straight to the thief's house collected all the stuff and brought it back to us. They also showed us a pot of animal fat that they picked up in the house of the thief as evidence of his intent. This was a brew of glandular fluids that the thief rubs over his arms and legs to stop the guard dogs barking. Apparently dogs love the smell and amorously lick the thief rather than bite him.

Caroline's infatuation with Rodge, as he became affectionately named, coupled with his good nature, led us to invite him and Griff to our house for

Christmas. Despite their age difference it was quite surprising how compatible they were.

In 1962 we had ten people to Christmas dinner with Christmas pudding and champagne. Rodgers sang Country and Western songs with his guitar, and under Caroline's influence we all twisted to exhaustion on the veranda in bright star-light.

Life in Mbeya was increasingly to our liking, we held a kind of open-house approach to society, which Jo's extrovert nature thrived upon. There was no 'standing on ceremony' as in England, people just turned up and bedded down. There was food and drink in exchange for a thank-you, for VSO's, Peace Corps, White Fathers, farmers, American anthropologists living in the bush, officials from Dar es Salaam. When in Rome, as they say, for it is the customary treatment of travellers in African society also.

Saturday curry lunch with lashings of cold beer, an Asian custom that we enjoyed, utilised the sunny garden atmosphere and attracted scores of expatriates. This occurred every Saturday somewhere in Mbeya, no invitations, the word got round as to where the gathering was taking place.

On Boxing Day at Home Farm in Norfolk we always had a big pheasant shoot. No pheasants in Tanganyika of course but there were much wilder versions of what in England we would call game birds namely kwali or spur fowl, because of their vicious spurs, sand-grouse in flocks of a million that live on open sandy plains, guinea fowl in flocks of two to three hundred, and an assortment of wild fowl on flood plains. The great joy of all this was the absence of bird shooting regulations, licences, closed seasons, and private land. Uhuru or freedom from colonial rule was fundamentally a return to previous greater freedoms of which we have lost sight of in the UK.

The place of our Boxing Day indulgence? Usangu plains in the Central Rift Valley, far from town and inaccessibly flooded from January to June. The flooding was not caused by rain on Usangu, which is rare, but the surrounding mountain streams. Thus the bird life gained natural seasonal protection from hunters.

Stretching 200 miles from Mbeya almost to Iringa, Usangu was the haven, not only of wildfowl but of herds of ungulates, grazers and their predators. The rich grazing also attracted nomadic Maasai following the rift valleys from the north. Usangu was a wonderful draw for self-reliant adventurers, campers, and hunters and we took every opportunity to get down there at week-ends with the family.

On Boxing Day before dawn, the Ford Zodiac and Eric and Jean's Standard Vanguard station wagon, were loaded up with camping gear, guns, dogs children and last but not least, wives, for a couple of days on Usangu. Rodgers unexpectedly produced a thirty-thirty calibre saddle gun and hunting licence. This was a double short-barrelled rifle of .30 calibre as used in the Wild West. I was a bit concerned about what use this weapon might be put to in the hands of an inexperienced young American who could not tell male from female animal, or which animals he would be permitted to shoot with a relatively light calibre bullet. Big Game hunting was strictly controlled by the Game Department.

We reached Marere's Boma at the beginning of Usangu, after one and a half hours drive, singing Western songs, and with Cocker Spaniel Sally straining at the leash as she became bathed in the glorious scents of the wild. The raucous singing stopped as we hit mud and spun helplessly. Eric was behind us, his car loaded with children and his Springer Spaniel Buster. Everyone jumped out and became instantly busy, jacking up the car and collecting brushwood to put under the wheels, whilst the two dogs coursed the area, maddeningly putting up kwali everywhere.

The rising sun already flooded the Ukinga mountains backdrop, first with red and then with gold light. With the vehicles stationary there was an uncanny chilly silence, but we knew that the sun would soon bring the plains to life. Once through the wet spot to dry ground we roped up to Eric's Vanguard and pulled him through and off for another hour across dry grey clay plain.

Suddenly the sky turned brown with sand grouse coming from the hills for water in the swamps. We stopped and stared in amazed fascination as they chortled with deep husky voices as though in conversation, perhaps about events below and the prospects at the waterhole, and what their sisters and brothers were up to. It was a mystery to us where they all came from in their thousands, as one only ever saw them at dawn and dusk, as though they had emerged from the earth like African spirits are reputed to do.

We walked across to the swamp margins and enjoyed sport the like of which we never knew in Norfolk. The spaniels too were delirious with excitement, not to mention the children, whom it seems the world over are uninhibited in their hunting instincts.

By 9.0 am we decided that our mini meat mountain would feed our families for weeks to come, and called it a day. There were six teal ducks, three Egyptian geese or gypies, three big old black spur-wing geese, five kwali, four whistling tree ducks, and fourteen sand-grouse.

Blood sucking midges were now taking toll of our tolerance. The flaming sun, now above the mountains flooded the reed beds with bright orange, heralding the impending heat of the day. Already a mirage made the distant vehicles appear to be floating above the ground.

We headed out towards the Bohoro Flats in search of bigger game taking care to avoid the deadly 'black cotton soils' where a car can sink and be lost for the rest of the rainy season. We intended to view the miracles of nature and not to shoot. The children sat on the roof racks in the breeze, as spotters. We touched 50 mph in places. A shout went up, 'Twiga, right, after them Dad.'

We gave chase for the fun of it. Giraffe seem to lollop along casually in a rocking horse gait, yet we were hard put-to to keep up with them, swerving, dodging thorn bushes and pot holes at 40 mph. The instant we stopped they stopped, and gathered round to goggle down at us as we became shrouded in our dense white dust.

'I'm not sure who the oddity is here!' I remarked as those look-alike beauties batted their eye lids and stared down their noses at the liquorice allsorts collection of humans, tin and wheels, and dogs.

Rodgers seemed to feel the need to assert his mighty American power and reached for his 30-30.

Caroline erupted, 'What do you think you're going to do Rodge, don't you know that to shoot twiga is illegal. Forget shooting. Think of this as a Broadway Show.'

I sensed echoes of her Iringa England versus America common knowledge exchange.

'Okay Miss Smarty Pants. Just habit,' said Rodgers defensively, 'but just imagine what they could do to our car, if they'd a mind to, and then where would we be, stranded, probably murdered by the Maasai.'

'What twaddle, why should they want to tread on our car, unless of course they knew that you were in it?'

Rodge's response was lost in the mirth of the rest of us.

The milometer was reading 80 miles from Mbeya. The heat was sapping our strength. We had counted 35 twiga. We made camp. There was a water hole in the otherwise dry river bed; it served to boil for our oddly flavoured tea. The hot air zizzed with jet propelled insects. Our fly sheet tied to the roof rack served as an admirable shade under which to scan the plains for signs of game. Nothing. Just a string of about 100 scrawny Zebu cows in the mirage.

Maasai? Yes a red blanket and long spear emerged distantly. We hoped he'd give us a wide berth.

Richard and I chased a flock of about 200 guinea fowl, .22 at the ready. They ran and ran this way and that, flew a bit, ran again, chortling noisily. We were soon out of sight of camp. The proverbial wild goose chase is nothing compared to a wild guinea fowl chase. We came close to getting lost in the white thorn bush moonscape and all for a kill success rate of a half of one per cent.

We set off to find elephants in the far away Rufiji Swamp. We were now a hazardously long way from any road. However I knew that we were close to the great migratory elephant circuit that I learned about from the Provincial Game Warden, David Ansty. This circuit goes for hundreds of miles through the vast Ruaha Game Reserve, later to become a National Park, passing North West towards of Kipembawe, then west to Rungwa valley and then south to Lake Rukwa and Mbeya hills.

We scattered herds of zebra, David Ansty said there were three thousand on Usangu. One happily stood and posed for us, perplexed at our black and white un-zebra-like shaped car.

'I've got a compass for the shortest route to the swamps, follow me.'

I revved my engine to drown doubters. Driving straight on a compass bearing is a fanciful idea, even on an open plain, there are concrete hard potholes where elephants passed last wet season, clumps of impenetrable thorn bush, erosion gullies and concrete termitaria about one foot high, enough to break an axle. Two hours later the Fahrenheit temperature and the milometer read 135.

A clump of big Acacia albida trees suggested water, shade and elephants. There was neither, and we were on the edge of our universe. We stopped to gulp down water only to be startled by a vicious looking black wart hog male with gleaming tusks that bolted from its wet mud hole, tail erect like a transmission aerial. Glad to say it was not in a confrontational frame of mind. The wart hog remained in view as it trotted relentlessly across from right to left along the mbuga. Rodgers could not contain himself, flinging himself down flat as though he was on Omaha beach on D Day, aimed and fired repeatedly, and wildly as Yanks do. His shots bit-the-dust all round the pig, but this muscular black Indebum did not; he just kept going and going and going, until he was out of sight. We all heaved a sigh of relief. Caroline showed admirable restraint, confining herself to a cold look. Silence prevailed as one red face returned for a sip of water.

The boys scanned the shimmering mirage. We were off again, disturbing a flock of colourful crested cranes and a secretary bird. We drew quite close and sensed in silence their minimum permitted distance, cameras cocked. They were cow sized beefy beasts with short horns spiralling straight upwards, however unlike any cow I knew these could jump like fleas when pursued by a black and white car.

Pursuing evidence of greenness to our left we came across an mbuga, and began walking through knee high grass. We were rewarded by finding a herd of topi. This was a first for us. Slightly smaller than a cow, they were odd looking, sloping down from head to tail, couldn't think why, but a deep mahogany colour with blue shoulder flashes and breeches, giving a touch of beauty to an otherwise awkward looking animal with crooked horns. Rodgers was heard to mutter, 'Next time I'll have one of those. Keep us in meat for six months.'

We gave up looking for elephants and turned for home. As we were spearheading a column of fine white dust, there came a call from the pilots on the roof rack;

'Look over there Dad there's a turkey.'

It was that size all right, and walked ponderously, in a sort of hesitant gliding motion, carrying its flat backed body level with the ground. Its long neck gave the large head that haughty look that the giraffe has. Its straight beak looked fearsome, its voice indescribably un-birdlike. Its guarded retreat and elevated look, gave it an air, Philip thought, of having been up to something. He should know!

'It's the Greater Bustard, Philip.' I shouted.

Philip later told our vicar that he'd seen, 'a great big bastard on Usangu.' The Reverend responded, 'Well Philip, let's hope he doesn't come to town.'

Everything seemed to be happening at once now; we counted forty prancing antelope, racing zebra, strolling crested cranes resplendent in their gorgeous plume head-dress, gawky twiga and black wart hogs racing away like trains. This was the Bohoro Flats; Jo called it the Bohoro Flats Ballet.

I confided to Jo, 'Did you notice those fresh elephant dung balls near the mbuga? One day you and I will come this way on our own in the Land Rover, and we'll just keep on going and going and going, like that warthog, until we get to Iringa. What do you think? A short cut; no-one's done it since Captain Elton the explorer crossed this way on foot in 1875, and died.'

'Fantastic. I'd love to. We'd need to be sure though, no petrol, no AA

Rescue. I know your short cuts. Remember those Roman roads you found on the map when the children were small, and we all ended up in a gated field in the dark!'

'Well,' I responded, 'It's a challenge.'

Italy, Camogli.

'Hey You, Mac Gregor, catch my line'

Port Sayid

Port Sayid, Jo and David Slater

Aden - ss.Kenya Castle 1962

Our guide in Aden

Aden, Caroline and Queen Victoria, looking towards her beloved India

Mombasa arrival 1962

Welcome to Africa, Jo

Philip age 7, tortoise age 100

Our first station Tengeru

Tengeru Job applicant

'Crazy bugger' pronounced Huw

Caroline on her thirteenth birthday

'A penny for your picture'

Village butcher's shop

We met Maasi by the roadside

Brian and Sally in Matwiga

Bwana Pima in Matwiga

Matwiga, Miombo woodland

Twiga in Matwiga

Not another brake failure!

Crack shots - Village boys

Morale boosters Jo and Sally

'Put on your African sandles Brian'

Garden Boy's garden boy

At the 'grassroots'

Lake Rukwa - Tiger Fish

Lake Rukwa, Caroline and the boys

Ecologically friendly ----------
Mule powered Morris Minor

On Lake Rukwa, Caroline, Richard and Sally

A hundred miles from nowhere, Usangu

Usangu, historically a man-eater hereabouts

'Twiga left!' shouted Richard from the car roof

Usangu, baby zebra

Samson after a guinea fowl supper

Usangu, Japanese de Villiers

Cheetah on Usangu

Guests for breakfast in Amboseli

Tukuyu; bananas 100 for a shilling

Tukuyu, we swam in Masoko volcano crater lake

Mbozi meteorite

Tukuyu, Mkwale plains

School bus, stearing track rod broke

Eric's Wedding Group

Eric's bride

The Coventry Knight 48 rescued and restored

Brian loves his soil pits! 'Look out for elephants'

Matwiga, tobacco trial plot

Jo skinny dipping in Ngualla volcano crater

'Chocolate Elephants' in Rungwa Valley

Jo darning the bridge on the way to Elton Plateau, re-named Kitulo

Jo sitting below a lava flow on Kitulo

Kitulo primaeval flora

Kitulo, Tim Harvard at 8700 ft altitude

Kitulo, 45 spp. of orchids, this is Disa wallerii

Ruaha, Steve flying the boys out game spotting

After flying with Steve, the river came from nowhere

Philip in Mbage Camp, Ruaha

Ruaha. 'Do you think we'll get home for Xmas, Dad?'

Oxfam came to the rescue

The family four years later, 1968

Chapter Nine

Dinosaur Eggs and Murder in the Camp

On New Year's Eve our usual evening pleasantry, a glass of cool Kilimanjaro lager on the veranda, was interrupted by the arrival of a Forestry Land Rover. It was Peace Corps Griff, from Alabama, tall dark, short cropped hair, bung-ho trigger-happy Griff.

'Beer, Griff?'

Jo looked at him with an impish smile crossing her face.

'That gash in the centre of your forehead Griff? Your students had you banging your head against a brick wall again?'

'Aw. That was the scope of my .375 rifle; it struck me between the eyes when I fired. Reckon I must have been tired. My tracker and I had been walking for two days looking for tembo.'

I butted in, 'You've been shooting elephants with a .375! And a telescopic sight!! I'm surprised the Peace Corps accepted you with eye sight that bad. What became of the poor old elephant? '

'By the time I came round there was no sign of it, or my tracker. Reckon he thought I'd shot me-self instead of the tembo and he might get charged with murdering a white man. Lucky I found my way to a village. Thought I'd fractured my darned skull. Anyway nothing on the X-ray plate. Wasted my leave though, and an elephant licence. You reckon a .375 is too light for tembo, its OK on the licence? Imagine what my head would be like with a heavier calibre!'

'I recall reading a book about the famous Edwardian elephant hunter in Uganda called Karamoja Bell. He spent his whole life killing elephants, so he knew all the tricks, and he used a .275 double barrelled Rigby, a really light weapon, but deadly accurate, the thing is, he only ever used the heart shot. You could never stop a charging elephant with a .375. Don't be suicidal Griff, stick to buffalo, plenty of 'em, and extremely challenging.'

'Well I'm looking for a challenge not a sore head.'

'Where'd you find those elephants, Griff?'

'Chunya District, towards Rungwa River in the West beyond Gua Mission. Long way out, tsetses were hell, covered my back like a woolly blanket at times. I really felt like a mobile burger bar. So Brian, where to your next safari?'

'We are doing a tsetse free excursion tomorrow to the Songwe River valley with the children, that is if I can drag Caroline away from her horse riding.'

As it turned out Caroline was attracted by the idea of bathing in the hot springs and it was Philip who was dragging his feet. I extracted a question from him about a fear of dinosaurs.

'What's this about dinosaurs, Philip?' Richard said.

I thought, hmm, here we go again.

'There are dinosaurs in Songwe Valley?'

There was, as ever, an element of truth in what Richard told him, it was just the tense he used, present for dramatic effect, past for reality. Richard had heard me talking about a village headman over in Njerenji near the Songwe telling me that they had found diamonds in the river, and also that his people knew of dinosaur eggs in the foothills. The latter I had later seen for myself, like huge stone ostrich eggs. I managed to put Philip's mind at rest, or so I thought, by impressing upon him that we were talking about pre-history.

However he then asked, 'Did you and Mum see any dinosaurs when you were little?'

'Er ... no, can't say we did. Tell you what though I met an African who told me that he had found diamonds in the Songwe river gravel. Do you fancy getting rich quick?'

Sally was in the car before breakfast. She always knew when it was Sunday.

We popped in to look at the Mbozi meteorite on the way and took photos. It stands about a quarter exposed, and is said to be the fourth largest in the world. It's just there, no formal recognition or protection, just a fifteen ton boring old lump in the bush. A local coffee farmer named Wilderboltz showed me a piece that he'd hack-sawed off. It was shiny metal and very heavy. He measured its displacement and weight then multiplied by the approximate physical size to get the estimated tonnage.

I remarked to the children that it was about the size of a five ton elephant. What made me think of that? Mental telepathy; we suddenly became aware of the deep rumbling sound of elephant, and beat a hasty retreat to the car.

'Right! Let's go!' Jo's alarm registered in the children's faces at once.

'It's come from outer space you know!' I said, 'I've got my geological hammer I could knock a bit off for you if you like.' Blank faces returned with youthful apprehension.

Caroline murmured something about always getting hung up on rocks when we're out in the bush. Suddenly an elephant appeared from nowhere right behind us and we hastily departed.

I now had a captive audience in the car as we headed for Songwe valley.

'You know - rocks and the bush can be dull until you've learned to read it, then everything around you has a story to tell.'

Just then a party of fat red throated kwali crossed the road in front of us.

Philip erupted, 'Ooh, look at them. What story do they tell you Dad?'

'They tell me ... it's nearly lunchtime. No seriously, I was telling you that the landscape is full of secrets about the past, which helps you to understand the present. Walking cross country is like a treasure hunt, looking for clues, everywhere there are indicators, signs. There's always a story hidden in the bush. The rocks tell you what the soil is like even without digging holes. The type of vegetation tells you the depth of the soils and the climate and whether the land has been cultivated recently and abandoned. The type and density of wild animals tells you whether the soil is acid and poor, like Kipembawe, or alkaline and rich in nutrients, like Usangu for example. The termite mounds tell you about the water table and the honey guide bird whether there are bees to fertilise the groundnut flowers on the farms.'

It was very quiet; I think they were listening, perhaps not?

'You can see why Alexander Maki refers to your dad as Professor Pima.'

We passed through a coffee plantation in full bloom, the scent was overwhelming and the windows came down to imbibe it. We hit the main road, over the Songwe Bridge, swung left into the lime-works drive and halted in front of the house. Our dust cloud caught up and enveloped us. The windows were hastily wound up again.

'Hello there. Come and have a cup of tea,' came a strident female voice from the open window.

Gisela was a bit surprised to see five of us, and a spaniel, troop into her sitting room and consume all the available furniture. A man in his mid-eighties, named Bunny Brown, sat in a dark corner. He had a reputation for affairs, for popping in and out of Mbeya and Chunya warrens of ladies boudoirs during the gold-rush days, like Falstaff in search of favours, hence his nick name Bunny.

Beefy 'Frau' Gisela must have been, or is, a mighty challenge for Bunny. What ever the truth of it, he is nowadays always found sitting, exhausted, in Geisha's corner.

I took my tape recorder along in case of some more of Gisela's glorious stories of times past. I was amply rewarded.

'My husband, who committed suicide by the way when Tanganyika declared Independence, was an Englishman, a pilot in the first world war. The British Government offered him a farm in Mbozi, after the war. He walked here from Nairobi. A few German farmers were still here by world war two so they were interned, at Njombe. There were a lot of them in the hills around there of course. Being married to an Englishman I was Okay.'

'I did wonder, I mean what happened to you during the war.'

Gisela continued unabated, 'Those Germans up there had lists of African chiefs to be hanged when Hitler won the war. Their tea estates were handed over to Brooke Bond, on lease. They've expanded now and produce top quality tea. They are a beautiful sight; I expect you've been up there Brian, with your job"

'Not yet. Government policy has taken a dramatic change, you know, I have to devote my whole time to African farmers, and forget about white farmers. So you were a farmer then Gisela?'

'I sold up and bought this mine for £100 off George Rushby, the man who killed the Njombe man-eating lions on Usangu. I make a living from selling polished travertine marble. It's beautiful stuff, lovely colours; I'll give you some to take home. Wish we had tourists round here. I also sell bat guano for fertiliser, from the caves. We've cut down about forty feet and still no sign of the bottom. It must have been a bats *choo* for a million years.'

After a cup of tea the children went off to explore, whilst we pursued

Gisela on the evergreen topic of African character.

'I must say, Africans are never vindictive like Europeans sometimes are. They are good scholars but absolutely no initiative, that's what holds them back ... can't seem to use their knowledge. They see education only as a means to attain status and an office to flounce in. I believe that life was never *really* hard here, as it was in Europe. Nature provides here. Also they believe that their destiny is pre-determined by their ancestral spirits, so no point in trying to take the initiative and risk the wrath of the Gods.'

I told her about my settlement scheme plans, what did she think?

'The townspeople depend upon the rural areas to feed them. A growing market means that the farmers must learn new tricks. The Wasafwa are doing this, trouble is they are soon put down if they get rich. The good thing about your scheme is that the settlers will be far away from their relatives and tribal culture. Let me tell you a true story, is your tape running?'

'Yes. Fire away.'

'I employed an enterprising Msafwa chap on my place a few years ago ... he took up modern deep litter egg production and made lots of money selling eggs in Mbeya. Then his relatives became jealous and organised a sorcerer to poison him, not too drastic, just enough to make him conform to their social rules. He finally went crazy and ended up in the asylum at Dodoma. However once he was away from the influence of the sorcerer he normalised, and eventually returned to his village. He never again took up any modern ideas of food production after that.'

'Tell them about Dr Erkhartz brother,' interjected Bunny.

'Oh yes! Dr Erkhartz, the Mbeya doctor, he had a brother working near Tabora who told the doctor that the prostitutes there never got pregnant. He said that they all wore a stone on a lace round their waists. He decided to charm one of his girl friends to be de-charmed. They don't mind having white babies actually. The stone was sent to his brother, who sent it to Germany for analysis. Guess what! The stone turned out to be radium.'

Sally appeared, heralding the return of the children.

'We've found a good picnic spot Mum.' Caroline said assertively.

'Clear the area of shrubs and grass, my dears,' Gisela advised, 'lots of snakes round here ... I must tell you Caroline ... the other night I came in here and trod on a black and yellow cobra, on the floor, just where you're standing ... it felt horrible under my foot, sort of gristly. I leapt in the air; I can tell you, yes me at 55 years old, right up onto that table in one leap. No need to worry though Caroline, they don't come in here when Mr Brown's sitting there in the corner!'

'Right! We'll be down there in five minutes.' Jo declared emphatically.

'Talking of snakes,' Gisela was in full spate again, 'the dogs were barking wildly one afternoon, and then my old cat started hissing so I knew there must be a snake about. I took the torch round my cupboards but, nothing. Then I saw it, under my bed, a huge python. Forgetting that I was barefoot I leapt out of the window and landed on some Jesus Thorn which set me yelling. The shamba boys came running and then fetched the men from the village with spears. They all crept into the house on tip toe, consumed with fear, then leapt on to the bed and plunged a long spear right through the mattress, spiking the python underneath. Believe me that python's strength was enough to bend that spear. They killed it and it measured fifteen feet long. Snakes can smell water in the house of course. My daughter first learned to walk by following a green mamba out of the house and across the lawn!'

Jo laughed, 'Do you know any stories about donkeys, Gisela?'

She had noticed the children listening in the doorway.

'As a matter of fact I do,' signalled a further distraction from our picnic, 'Bunny hasn't heard this either, it was a good many years ago mind you ... this man who stayed with us one night, traded regularly up and down from Sumbawanga on the border to Chunya, taking the short cut across Rukwa valley near Galula salt pan. I spent 4½ years digging salt pans there in my youth ... it used to be 3½ days walk to Mbeya from Galula if you got snake bite ... oh sorry ... this man used a donkey to carry his trade goods. On the way back he stayed here again. Our house was roofed with Mbozi tiles which are very heavy indeed. Well ... he tied his donkey to the corner wooden pillar near the veranda and off-loaded. There was honey, beeswax and smoked Tilapia ... you could smell him coming a mile off, and I reckon the lions could too. About midnight there was pandemonium and the roof collapsed over the sitting room. A lion had taken the donkey and pulled the pillar down that it was tied to.'

We were laughing when Bunny interjected with a serious note, 'That trader died of black-water fever actually. Hundreds did in those days. Kidney failure you know, causes black urine. Quinine was the only malaria treatment we had and it caused kidney failure. We didn't know the cause then. The man's name was Hallyer.'

The children had gone in frustration.

'Just one last question for the tape Gisela, how did you get here in the first place?'

'I came here in the early 20s when I was Caroline's age, with my sister and parents. We came from Dar es Salaam in a Ford 4, a bit more basic that your Ford Brian, it had wooden wheels and solid tyres. Good for almost non-existent roads mind you, no punctures. The natives used to gather round and carry the car over the rivers. We set up farm at Mbozi, planted coffee, and then in the third year the bush fires caught us and we went bankrupt. After two years starvation, my parents and sister went back to Europe and I married my Englishman. Then when I had my daughter I had to walk to the mission when my labour started. It was 25 miles ... I shall never forget that.'

After our picnic we finally set off on foot down the valley, pushing through four foot tall grass along the river. We spotted the blue flash of fleeting kingfishers. An overhead clapping caught us out every time, we looked up to see that it was only the huge leaves of the borassus palms responding to an uplift of the hot air, as though applauding our progress.

We only dabbled in the steaming springs. The offensive sulphurous odour repelled us from previous ambitions to indulge in a secluded swim. The surrounding rocks were 'frosted' over with crystalline deposits. We could not help but reflect upon what a wealth of touristy attractions Mbeya had to offer the world; volcanoes, lakes, wildlife, trout fishing, dramatic scenery, a rare meteorite, hot springs and dinosaurs. One day perhaps.

'Over there, under that cliff the other side of the river is where I found the dinosaur eggs. They were about ten inches long. Everything round here seems to be associated with sedimentation, hot springs, marble, salt pans and clay beds, fossilised dinosaur eggs.'

Caroline said, 'Those eggs probably got caught in some great flood, like swans' eggs do sometimes at home.'

'Philip wants to go paddling for diamonds. You other two must go with him and keep watch for crocs, please.' said Jo.

We climbed up to some rocks and sat together keeping watch and reflecting upon the dramatic scenery of the rift valley.

'No sign of villages or cultivation for some reason. Wonder if the Rungwe volcano will ever blow its top again and blanket the land with hot ash like it did before so many times. They ought to monitor the temperature of these hot springs really, as a precaution.'

'Jo. My geological map shows a disused niobium mine over there, which reminds me of something that Bunny Brown said about gold. That stream over there falling over the Sumbawanga escarpment. Bunny says it carries alluvial gold. Here, take a look with the binoculars. See that bowl in the rock about half way down?'

'Yes, the water sort of boils over it.'

'Right. There's our pension. You know how heavy gold is!'

'A pot of gold! Brilliant! You know everything Brian!'

Alexander Maki burst into my office the day following our excursion to the Lime Works with news of a jealous assault in our survey camp. He had had a difficult 27 hours careful journey from Matwiga in torrential rain.

'Good morning Bwana. Bad news I'm afraid, please come.'

In the back of his Land Rover lay Velentino Sebastiani with a stab would just above the heart. His assailant, I was told, was chainman Yahaya, who was secured with a forlorn look on his face, in the cab. I procured the attention of our young British doctor at the hospital while Yahaya was admitted to the other place with bars, to await the outcome of emergency treatment for Valentino.

The story went that Yahaya was in Mbeya with the others at the month end, for their wages, food, and family. Valentino remained in camp on watch. He ran out of sugar and 'borrowed' from Yahaya's food box. When Yahaya returned he became angry and accused Valentino the senior man, of stealing. The old tribal hatreds arose to inflame the language on both sides, terminating in an attack with a long bread knife. Valentino's life now hung on a thread.

Four weeks later, Valentino died, despite having made good progress on daily lung drainage. It appeared there was some neglect at the hospital in the form of a missed daily draining. This news added annoyance to my grief. Yahaya was charged with and convicted of murder. His sentence was 18 months prison. I was not impressed, considering cattle theft carried a minimum sentence of seven years.

Life is cheap in Africa, I thought. Children die of malnutrition and preventable diseases, adults commonly from wild creatures, malaria, sleeping sickness, water borne parasites, bacteria, witchcraft, and AIDS. There is an attitude of inevitability about death when something goes wrong in their tribal communities.

I organised a funeral for my best surveyor. My staff and friends chipped in for the sixty shillings required for a box. There were no relatives at the funeral. Valentino came from a thousand miles away in the north east. They probably didn't know of his demise.

Jo and I were shocked and saddened by this turn of events, and sat on the veranda that evening, quietly pondering upon how such a minor incident could have such a dramatic outcome.

It was now January and the swallows were in and out from under our eaves feeding their young. Jo commented on their instinctive need to rear two broods every year by flying all the way to England.

'They must feel insecure in Africa. Not sure where their home is .... like us really.'

Chapter Ten

Rain, Rain, Go Away

Mike Hickson-Wood promised Mbeya bird shooters, one last larder-stocking wild fowl trip to Usangu Plains. We thought that we had seen the last of Usangu for five months now that the rains had started. The valley plains rarely receive rain but the surrounding mountains jettison their surplus into the rift valley to form swamps that attract wildlife in abundance. Mike knew his way around the Southern Highlands better than anyone, even me. His father had been on the Lupa Goldfields during the gold-rush in the 1920s. He was passionate about wild places and had purchased a new Toyota four wheel drive station wagon to enable him to explore the remotest corners, in which this part of Africa abounds. As a Land Rover enthusiast I expressed scepticism. Mike was determined to prove his resourcefulness and that of his new Japanese vehicle. No-one else would chance loosing their vehicle on the rapidly flooding plains of Usangu. Mike was not a shooter; he just loved a challenge, and popularity.

Mankind, we were told by Dr Leakey who discovered the earliest Homos in Olduvai Gorge in Tanganyika, that the first humans learned to walk on two legs on the flood plains of Serengeti. Thus he overcame his lack of good killing faculties, such as long canines, claws, and speed, by becoming bi-pedal. He could now see long distances, carry weapons, and meat back to his family. Usangu was just such a place and it still seemed a natural magnet to bipedals with weapons, and now with four wheels to boot. However wheels do have some limitations in January on the wet clays that resembled bars of soap. How different are tropical clays to the sticky English variety that claw, draw and drag at one's wheels. The Usangu grey clay presents a vehicle with no more hindrance than a skid pan.

Because of the risks, our wives were abandoned in town to congregate over coffee, and offer each other condolences over their estrangement at the hands of the Devil Usangu. Or was that wishful thinking?

It was at 5.45 am when we lurched to a halt at Marere's Boma on the edge of the plains. It was still dark, chilly, and desolate. This was when one asked oneself, why desert one's Venus in favour of Diana?

This location was the fortified palace of Chief Marere when in1877 explorer Captain James Elton took refuge here from the murderous warrior Machinga tribe who massacred eighty women outside its walls in order to draw the Wasangu defenders out from their boma. Terrorist tactics are nothing new it seems. They did not succeed. Now a farmer was the only resident and he had no tribal affiliations. His wiry frame appeared in the doorway. He was half oriental in appearance and dusky skinned, he was called Japanese de Villiers. He lived between three worlds, African, European, and Asian. He was forced to be immensely self-reliant. How did he survive? How did he come to be here? What was his genealogy? Did he sleep in that broad brimmed hat? He was generous with information about Usangu but not about de Villiers.

'Marnin Sars,' his voice was high pitched, 'you looking for nyama? I'll get my tractor ready to pull you out... for a small fee a course.' He grinned slyly, 'By de way, simba kep me up all night with his roarin. Fluds driving him this way. Better look out though.'

Chris Groocock, our young affable Mbeya vet handed Japanese two bottles of Tusker lager.

'Have a beer on us. See you later, bout eleven-ish I should think.'

His leathery face became all folds and teeth, 'Enjoy!'

I managed to take a photograph of this enigmatic character.

After a while the swamps came into distant view but the approach was simply a mirror of sun polished mud. We slid this way, that way, sideways, and even backwards at times. The essence of progress was to gain velocity on the dry spots and shoot the greasy mirror. It was fortunate that Mike had water-proofed the electrics since the Toyota was soon wading in a foot of water with a great bow wave building up ahead. Lunacy is less evident in a crowd.

After a while the water became too deep. We halted and the three spaniels jumped out and swam. We shouldered our guns for wading. 300 yards further on we paused in a huddled group at the edge of the swamp and gazed back at our escape module. It seemed to be floating on a white lake that stretched from sunrise to sunset.

'Don't worry it's only a mirage,' grinned Mike.

In that wild place we were about to noisily disturb nature's business of a million years for countless thousands of wildfowl. There were huge flocks of little waders, ponderous white storks, and the small red-billed teal that shoot up into the air almost vertically with phenomenal acceleration, vociferous Egyptian geese, ducks and geese of many species. Suddenly the sky was filled with white birds, fluttering against the grey sky like ticker tape at a New York carnival. They swirled higher and higher, out of range, seemingly preparing to leave the swamps.

We waited pensively, hoping they would change their minds and settle back into the reeds. They did, just out of gunshot. Whistlers came over first. These mahogany coloured white faced tree-roosting ducks fly like starlings in great flocks, whistling in a chorus of, 'shoot me if you can!'

Three hours and three exhausted spaniels later, we had shot and collected a few birds each. Enough is enough we agreed. Our skins were white and spongy with wading in warm water, our limbs weighed down with birds and the spaniels mouths choked with wet feathers. It all seemed to signal, 'time gentlemen please'. It was 10 am.

Eventually we reached the Land Cruiser and looked back. There could have been 10,000 white birds there, seeming in the mirage to be piled on top of each other like a mountain of snow in a tropical swamp. We were happy that abundance prevailed.

It was a relief when the engine fired, and a satisfied grin spread across Mike's face. We floated, swayed, rolled and rocked our way homeward. It was a long way. Fatigue set me dozing and dreaming of those January Norfolk marshes on wildfowling dawns in cutting east winds, where treacherous icy mud holes were death-traps for the unwary. After hours of numbing expectancy of, on a good day, sighting perhaps twenty greylag geese and with luck a flight of six or eight duck flashing by in the teeth of the gale. That old-timer Gisela was right when she told us that in her opinion, conditions for Africans are not that hard.

'Nature provides,' she had said.

One cannot actually imagine what coldness and deprivation feels like when hunting for food in such a steamy heat. It occurred to me that there was no incentive for an African to think and plan ahead and prepare for adversity.

We changed from floating to waltzing, the engine alternately roaring with spinning ineffective wheels, then grabbing the ground and lurching us forward. It was touch and go. We passed a local herdsman who leaned on his staff and gazed at the extraordinary quixotic load of lolling *Wazungu*, their white legs knee deep in wet ducks, feathers, spaniels, plimsolls and clinking empty beer bottles.

Back in Mbeya we were dropped off at our respective homes, like a fishmonger delivery service, each circumspect wife receiving one floppy, soft, grinning male, in a muddy hat, swinging a gun and a bundle of feathers plus a barely recognisable spaniel, bouncing up and down joyfully alongside. A clunky lunch bag was dropped on the veranda with a cheery wave and a 'Byeee!' from the departing triumphant Mike.

The next day, Monday, heralded another very African marathon Regional Development Committee. Amongst all the oratory was a gem of information for me, thus vindicating the quasi-African approach to my settlement scheme planning. The RDC allocated me £13,500 under the Regional Commissioners vote for 'mapping of resources and planning new schemes'. I was astounded. It was back to the drawing board, and sandals. The new Regional Commissioners name was Waziri Juma.

He later became a UN representative.

The RDC's thinking on the Elton Plateau UNDP proposed wheat and wool sheep scheme, was totally negative They thought vaguely that only Europeans could survive the cold up there and they were welcome to it. I was convinced also that some of them feared the Wambuda sect, prevalent in the mountains, who murdered people dressed as leopards.

The water table was now at ground level everywhere so field survey work was difficult. I decided to make that three day muddy drive to Dar for discussions with my technical boss Don Chambers. Also there was a bunch of birthdays coming up and nothing to buy in Mbeya.

In Dar es Salaam I found just the thing for Philip's eighth birthday. The Indian called it a *maridadi bunduki*, in English, a snazzy shiny toy rifle, a replica of my Browning .22 with a telescopic sight. It fired reels of caps so I made an urgent request to my mother in her 57th birthday card for reels of caps to be secreted in rolls of comics for Phil's birthday surprise. The authorities were very touchy about importing fireworks.

My shopping spree included Ladybird books and for Caroline a lovely bracelet with mini-African animals made from 97% pure silver. The Indians made these from Marie Theresia coins dated 1780 which were the currency on the coast in those days. I thought Jo would love the hand bag made from a man-eating lion with a black mane. Finally a native carved ebony walking stick for Jo's father Arthur, to use when walking his much loved Border Collie. My extravaganza did not cease there, there were zebra skin wallets for the folks back home, belts, native drums, bows and arrows, and a beautiful egg sized Sri Lankan moonstone for my sister Joy. I then discovered a glorious wall-consuming print of an elephant, one of the artist's early dynamic animal scenes depicting a bull elephant flapping its ears at the viewer, with Kilimanjaro in the background. It was quite a magnificent piece of the wild imagery by a little known artist, at the time, David Shepherd. I fell in love with this print and paid 130 shillings for it.

Don Chambers had done his best to secure ministry funds for resettling Wenela Repatriates at Kipembawe without success. He told me that the ministry would only consider assisting Virginia tobacco growing on European owned farms. This was the same philosophy that prevailed in Rhodesia where Africans were not considered technically and financially capable of coping with the huge brick barn curing process for Virginia tobacco. I felt that I could design a small simple curing system adapted to small scale production, using miombo woodland for fuel, oil drums for flues and mud and wattle buildings, which if they got burnt down would cost nothing to rebuild. It was no surprise to me that a government department was too demoralised to be innovative. It was the same in UK.

As to uplifting that proposed World Food Programme free food that John English had organised from Dar to Kipembawe, I found a new office in town called Oxfam. I had a word with them and found that, because Kipembawe was registered as being in a famine area in colonial times, they might be able to help with the transport of food. I was like a dog with two tales when I set off for home. Free food was not enough on its own of course but it was the thin end of the wedge for my struggle with the ministry. I loaded up the boot of my Zodiac with spare parts and coconuts, and left.

By March the rains were tailing off, giving us pleasant green days. The 27th was Philip's eighth birthday and there were several parcels from England. My sister always sends good gifts, this time it was an electric Mini-minor car. There was ten shillings for Richard whose birthday was in four weeks time. With a competitive edge looming, Richard rushed down to the dukas in search of a car and returned with a tin Mercedes from Japan, with lights. Furious East African Safari races round the garden ensued for the rest of the Easter holidays.

The following day Jo was heard to knowingly say to the boys, 'By the way, Richard, what happened to those reading books from your Grandma and Aunty Jean?'

'Oh ... I put them in their proper place Mum, on the bookshelf.'

Mbeya was hardly the sort of place where boys were tempted to sit indoors reading! Caroline too spent all her holidays outdoors, swimming, horse riding and socialising with her friend Kay Larlham. President Nyerere's recent ban on television was no great inconvenience either.

With Caroline home for Easter we loaded up the Mark III Ford Zodiac with camping gear on the roof rack and three children and one dog on the back seat, and headed south across the Mporoto volcanoes, the tribal home of the Wasafwa. Their misty village gardens were a delight of pyrethrum flowers and greenery. Owing to the cool mountain climate, what the Wasafwa call Irish potatoes, introduced by an Irish missionary in the 1930s were flourishing, also European vegetables which the women head-loaded profitably to Mbeya market. Wasafwa huts were pretty basic, with grass roofs steaming from the rain and their cooking fires inside. Although the rains had finished on the north side of the mountains, it was still raining on the south side. From that clammy cold place we were glad to descend through lush, exotically scented coffee plantations, to the steaming heat of Tukuyu town, which lay in the rift valley above Lake Malawi.

The hot tar road was steaming as we explored the colourful Tukuyu market, pressing amongst African women, well dressed in colourful fitenge cloths from under their arms to their knees, simply wrapped round and tucked in, quite often sporting portraits of President Julius Nyerere upon their prominent bottoms. The women were straight backed and elegant from carrying head-loads. In contrast to the Wasafwa mud wattle and grass huts, the Wanyakusa houses were square built with baked bricks and corrugated iron roofing.

We purchased a whole stem of bananas for a shilling, there must have been fifty. We also bought a box of pineapples for 20 cents, about 1/5th of a shilling.

This found Caroline calculating, 'Mom! Do you realise that for the price of a tin of Heinz Baked Beans in Mbeya we could buy... er... we'd need a lorry!'

Perhaps not the most intelligent remark from me;

'I could live on bananas when I'm on safari.'

This prompted Jo to respond, 'Great idea. Samson can stay home and cook for me in future.'

The Wanyakusa staple diet was bananas, and their countryside was a vast forest of plantains, high enough to build their huts beneath. Wanyakusa men had cars and their savings, from working in South African gold mines, were invested in cattle. There was every indication of that hackneyed adage that bananas feed the brain, was true. The government, business and the Civil Service were, in fact, substantially populated with Wanyakusa.

We met the Tea Officer. He told us that there was a Brooke Bond tea estate hereabouts, on upper slopes near the escarpment and he would take us there. First of all he conducted us round the old German Boma. It was a spooky old place like a French Foreign Legion outpost. It was explained to us that the Germans hadfixed the plumbing in the boma so that they could listen to the conversations in the officer's quarters, through the plug hole. Any criticism of the Empire or the German hierarchy was dealt with in the usual Teutonic way - ruthless severity. In 1910 they had a telegraphic link with the coast!

We drove up to the Brooke Bond tea estate for a fascinating tour of the factory. I took a photograph of the children plucking green tea leaves. Constant plucking had produced a table top shape to the dark green bushes making the whole mountainside look pleasantly smart and tidy, like an English country estate.

Below Tukuyu we drove constantly downwards through a veritable banana forest, smoke trailing skywards from the canopy indicating huts beneath. But mosquitoes soon made their hideous presence felt, enjoying the ten feet of rain per year. There is nowhere on earth more amenable to a mosquito than a banana grove. The suffering cattle stood round smoking fires to get some relief.

We made camp down on Lake Malawi shore to catch the breeze. We soon took to beach combing as we always did on the Norfolk coast, probably another of those evolutionary primeval instincts associated with the lake shores of East Africa's cradle of mankind. We found two German hella coins and popped them into a cup of Coke. They came up like new. The markings were clear - Deutsche Ostafrika, 1910.

Next day we headed for Masoko volcano crater lake where some imaginative colonial District Commissioner had sited a government rest house overlooking the water. This remarkable site is an extinct volcano filled with rain water. As it happens it was the closest point to the Mkwali Plains below the Livingstone Mountains where I had been directed by the RDC to survey and plan a scheme for the Tukuyu unemployed to grow rice. Whether they had the know-how or the disposition, no-one knew. This was the third such political scheme I had been conscripted into.

We arrived at Masoko rest house in the dark, lit the pressure lamps and set up our camp beds and mosquito nets. There was rudimentary furniture which seemed luxurious and enabled us to play Totopoly whilst Jo cooked something on the primus, before we set about the fruit from Tukuyu market. In the morning light and at breakfast on the balcony, we were staggered to behold the most fantastic scenery around us. 'Whoever built this place had aesthetic taste. It certainly wasn't an African according to Caroline.

Immediately below us lay the volcano crater lake, still, darkly reflecting the black rain clouds that seemed to be pouring out of the mother of all volcanoes, Rungwe. That godly peak that created the topography as we see it today loomed broodingly over every other peak in the mountain ranges.

'Do the Africans actually swim in that black lake, Dad? Looks grim! Quite scary.'

'I don't think so Caroline. I can tell you that the defeated Germans from Tukuyu threw their gold bars and money into this lake before they left. People often dig up buried Roman treasure in Britain for the same reason. Africans here say there is an evil monster in this lake; wouldn't be surprised if the Germans put that rumour about to stop anyone going after their gold. A geologist told me it was two kilometres deep; so not much chance of get-rich-quick here.'

Down to the right of our breakfast table the land fell away gently to the distant twinkling amethyst sea of Lake Malawi, flanked by the 7,500 foot high escarpment wall, that rises skywards to be shrouded in the clouds of the mysterious lost world of the Elton Plateau.

Jo dropped me off by the River Kiwira.

I shouted back to her, 'Look's like there's more rain to come,' pointing at Rungwe, 'if the river rises in flood, I might have a problem returning. Don't worry I'll get back sooner or later. I can walk up to the rest house.'

I jumped into a dug out canoe, ferrying a lady with a huge head-load of firewood. She squatted in the centre of the precariously rolling dug-out as we paddled out into the raging current. The slightest misjudgement by our helmsman and that lady would have drowned. I couldn't afford to be nervous alongside such a lady.

Whilst I was away Jo met our VSO Tim Smith, doing his agricultural rounds of gardens near Masoko market. She brought him up to the rest house to meet the family. She remarked that he looked pale.

He said jokingly, 'It's probably due to living under the banana canopy. It doesn't seem to have that effect on the Wanyakusa though!'

Tim was a most unassuming character, so unlike the brash Peace Corps, in fact quite the gentleman, and the family took him to heart at once. After introductions there was discussion about the possibility of ignoring African superstitions, and swimming in the Crater Lake.

'Must be free of bilharzia, that's one good thing,' he said.

'Good point. The vector snails need shallow water vegetation, I believe, and these vertical walls go straight down to nowhere, I'd say.'

Caroline's eye brows rose and her jaw fell, 'You can count me out.'

'I'm game,' Tim chimed in, 'how about you Jo?'

'Right...' Not quite the same as Okay.

Meanwhile I had found a natural bridge along the Kiwira River which appeared to be a volcanic lava flow undermined by the river. I was home in time for tea, and a swim.

The children watched as we three adults slithered down the steep pathway to the dark water. There was a lava boulder at the water's edge, without which we could not have got out again! The children were above us in the sky watching. No room for trepidation in front of the children. In we plunged. Wonderfully chill, in fact quite icy. Our splashing echoed round the walls in an otherwise eerie silence.

Suddenly we became alarmed at the way we all seemed to be drawn towards the middle.

'Horrible feeling there being no bottom to this lake!' burbled Jo.

'Can't be that deep otherwise it would be warmed by the centre of the Earth.' I quipped.

'Oh, that's all right then, Tarzan,' shouted Jo as she struck out boldly for the middle. After some ten yards she turned and swam back, 'Brian! I'm getting out.'

Her voice sounded different.

'Come over and give me a push, I'll get the kettle on for tea.'

Bang went my plan for a late skinny dip with Jo, yet again, defeated by monster hippos at Rukwa and now a monster of the deep here.

After dinner we offered Tim a game of Totopoly by lamp light to fill the long dark evening, but he hesitated.

'It's just that I'm worried about that black sky. My silly moped is not designed for muddy slopes. I'd never make it back to my hut if it rains. Tell you what; I'll come up tomorrow as soon as the sun dries things out a bit. Thanks all the same. So I'll be off then. Cheerio!'

Tim knew what he was talking about. I had no sooner put out my rain gauge than there was a tic-tack on the tin roof, followed by a faint hiss. Someone with a sense of humour said,

'Sounds like the cat spat on the hot tin roof.'

The note changed to a patter.

'Close the doors and windows here it comes.'

The pressure lamps barely repelled the intense darkness. The hiss of the lamps was soon drowned by the deafening roar of rain on the tin roof. We could not even speak audibly. Jo picked up the torch and peered out. Water was running across the forecourt in sheets. We felt like Noah as the downpour swelled unceasingly into the night.

After a sleepless night of deafening uncertainty, Jo reversed her previous opinion about the colonial DC having aesthetic taste.

'He must have had a corrugated mind that man.'

A bright sunny morning drew us from our steaming tea cups to a steaming world outside. Professor Dawtrey led his luckless pupils to the rain gauge for enlightenment, and declared,

'A precipitate of …. err … thirteen and three quarter inches! That's half as much as we got in a whole year back at Home Farm!'

'That's because, on the farm, Philip used to use the rain gauge to water his guinea pigs,' chimed in Caroline.

'What...?!'

Peels of laughter.

The Professor changed the subject to the refreshing view.

'The air's clear after that rain isn't it. Just look down there at Malawi, an azure mantle of sequins.'

'Look at those white storks,' Caroline changed the subject pointing upwards, 'There are hundreds.'

They were spiralling upwards on the thermals, ever higher and higher, and smaller and smaller until at 8,000 feet they resembled snow flakes in the hot blue sky. We watched them and as the leaders reached about 9,000 feet they swept north over the Elton Plateau and disappeared.

The Professor tried again, 'They do say, that the white storks float all the way to Holland, 6,000 miles, without flapping their wings. How's that for economy and brilliant aerodynamics. We've got a lot to learn from nature. We've got the Comet IV that can fly the same route, but it has to stop for fuel a couple of times, and you need a year's wages to buy a seat.'

'I wonder why they go all that way,' enquired Philip. He always asked questions.

'They gorge themselves on grasshoppers here and then nest on the Dutch chimney pots, and have their babies there. I suppose the cats can't get their chicks that way! They just have to make sure the chicks can fly before they leave the nest otherwise it's a long drop.'

'So looks like grasshoppers are an aphrodisiac,' said our teenager with a smirk.

Jo had been busy with her safari special - bacon and eggs.

'Come on you guys special breakfast for a special day.'

'Special day?!'

We were all stunned into silence for a moment.

'It's the twelfth of April, Mum's birthday!' we chorused.

There was a rush to all corners of the rest house. A small pile of cards and parcels materialised on the breakfast table, ensued by a rowdy heartfelt rendering of the song that all children love to sing. The grandest gift was the black-maned lion skin hand bag. That produced gasps of incredulity and thoughts of those man-eaters of Usangu. Jo subsequently carried her hand bag in the market producing a quiet air of reverence amongst the traders, though we thought that they inched their prices up for the mighty man-eating Memsab with the man-eating lion.

We were supposed to return home that day, and after loading the Zodiac in hot sunshine we piled in and drove out to the uphill roadway. The road was steaming red clay. I couldn't believe that I was in first gear, for we were going backwards.

'It's worse than I thought,' I declared with some embarrassment, 'We'll have to wrap nylon ropes round the tyres; it's like a bar of soap.'

I carried everything for emergencies.

'It'll take me some time so you can all get out.'

They never did get back in. I could not move the car at all on that slippery wet surface, so we resigned ourselves for a day's extension to our stay, and a prayer that it would not do it again.

The boys fished the Crater Lake with spinners and caught a good bream, which was fortuitous since all we had left was corn flakes, dried milk powder and the remains of the fruit from Tukuyu market. The fish was eyed with some suspicion. Was there any evil influence? Apart from the incredibly steely scales, the like of chain-mail, we felt that round two of our struggle with the forces of nature, went to us.

We had a guest for birthday tea served on the table outside, Tim Smith. He arrived on foot and declared, when he saw the giant bowl of chopped pineapples and bananas, and the Crater Lake fish, and the green Brooke Bond tea that we were, 'like a bunch of missionaries living off the land.'

That we were missionaries was true in a sense, though our soul food was not faith in God but in fundamental human motivation.

When we arrived back in Mbeya our friend Jean appeared almost at once, with a steaming airline grip.

'Look what I've found, take-away curry! Come round and have some.'

She told us that that morning the Dakota had been spotted, attracting acquisitive hunter-gatherers of the female gender. The hunter-gatherers had followed each other along the main street from duka to duka, surreptitiously peering into each others' shopping baskets. One or two had brought covert zip-bags for secrecy. Jean had discovered cheese!

There was some anxiety that if the Hindis noticed some sign of a rush that they would double their prices. So the ladies hatched a plan over lunch.

'I'll go ahead and search while you follow in the car with the bags. I'll signal by blowing my nose when I find something,' said one.

In due course a second birthday tea was arranged for both families to celebrate Jo's 34th year and her inner and outer beauty, so spoke I. We enjoyed the luxury of real cheese and real butter, instead of the ubiquitous slimy Blue Band Margarine. Eric joked about Jo's ability to thrive under bush conditions.

Chapter Eleven

Religious Factors and a Nuptual Occasion

With the boys still on Easter school hols, and the retreating rains yielding a fresh green habitat, I decided to take the boys on a bush whacking safari to my usual working haunt, Mazimbo survey camp in Matwiga. I dropped Jo off at the Outspan en route.

I decided to head for the main hill again, certain that wild dogs would not put in a second appearance. Uninhabited monotony did I say? Not so! There were native tribes who garrisoned every small rocky hillock and ant hill. Despite fatigue after the three mile walk, the boys decided to mount an attack on the highest hill fort. Like storm troopers they went in, waving sticks, throwing stones and laughing in derision, as they scattered the defenders. The wily enemy did not retreat far, just out of stoning range, the warrior males sat and barked back insults at us, baring their teeth whilst the females gathered their wayward families about them. If they had possessed as much aggression as my boys they could easily have overwhelmed us, there were so many.

The troop soon settled down to a watching game. The big dominant male drew closer and showed his disdain by urinating against a tree nearby. I caught him on film. Like the Ancient Greeks this tribe had a philosopher, a big male which sat on top of a giant ant hill as high as a house, in a posture of deep thought.

'I know of that posture. He's like me he looks to the bush for inspiration.'

My camera clicked again.

'It's my ambition to replace these thieving troops of baboons by thousands of enterprising humans. They'll grow maize and tobacco in grouped villages.' I told the boys, as we sat on the hill top like Celtic chieftains surveying the forest canopy, 'There'll be good houses, a school, a clinic, a duka and lots of shambas.'

'The baboons'll love that!' was Philip's prediction. 'They really go for mealies. And what about the elephants? They'll knock the houses down.'

Like a train driver Philip was always inspired by size and power.

'Elephants certainly pass this way on their circuit to Rungwa valley. You're right elephants mean trouble. But they're intelligent and with enough people settled here they'll learn to go round, I hope. They don't raid those banana forests where we were last week.'

Scattered about the canopy were protruding rocky outcrops, that the geologists call, to my mind poetically, meta-volcanic hills, like look-out posts, for the indigenous tribes of baboons. We sat dipping into our snack bag, speaking quietly in reverential tones in the utter silence of the undisturbed thousand square miles of forest at our feet.

'Last time I was here, I came across a harem of sable antelope. The big male was a handsome black and white fellow with four foot long shiny black horns curving over his back. Fantastic sight, I wouldn't like to meet him in the dark mind you. If we move quietly we might come across them, with the green grass everywhere. Shall we move?'

We must have covered seven miles by the time we reached Mazimbu camp, and not a murmur of complaint from the boys. We relaxed by the fire to an evening orchestration by falsetto piping tree frogs and tenor resonance from the mbuga swamp frogs. The choir was supported by the mighty basso profundo from Bufo regularis, toads. The fireworks display was provided by a myriad fireflies zipping to and fro in their desperate dash to attract females before sunrise, much as teenagers might do on motor cycles in the concrete jungles of Europe. I had a thought, 'Who needs television?'

The surveyors chatted incessantly as always, round the camp fire.

Thinking us out of earshot my driver said, 'If you ask the Bwana Pima where he's going? He always says... I don't know til I get there.'

Thomas Athumani looked puzzled, 'I can't see the point of it all, I mean all his college education, and the bwana still has to walk all day in the porini.'

This word porini is somewhat derogatory. The African considers the forest is for uncivilised people, a place of evil spirits and backward tribes, and baboons.

My surveyors knew our boys well and enjoyed their company. They were fascinated by our two boys' industrious, resourceful, and friendly disposition. The Africans responded by teaching them Kiswahili words, and how to survive in the porini, how to catch small birds, and mammals, how to collect and cook fat caterpillars - avoiding those with stinging protective hairs. Catching fish in traps immersed in the Mkowiji stream, fascinated them. They also learned to make a small cooking fire and to roast sausage flies, which are termites fattened for their nuptial flight. One can never get away from sex and killing in the porini and lastly, how to prevent snakes getting into their sleeping bags.

Contrary to school reports I found both boys extremely industrious, competent, and quick to learn and an asset in hazardous situations, which is more than can be said of a lot of adults! Especially those that Columbus invented, according to Caroline.

On our final day at Matwiga we awoke to that mysterious distant, muffled, thumping sound that often echoes through the miombo at dawn. I had at last identified it as the ground hornbill, a turkey sized black bird with a huge long bill and a red face. Like the cock pheasant, it is a reluctant flier, especially in woodland and communicates with deep whooping sounds rather like the bittern hidden in the Norfolk reed beds, also a recluse. Frequent efforts to sight the bird failed because it is something of ventriloquist and is never where you think it is.

At the week-end I headed for the boys' favourite watering hole, Lake Rukwa. On our long drive south we met white storks in their hundreds, flying north with the rains, just as the swallows do. They seemed to use the road as an airstrip, so that we had to drive through the flock.

Jo was waiting for us at the Outspan. The boys and I immediately cast our spinners for the challenging tigers.

Jo had a pleading look in her eye, 'Hey you, forget about tiger fish, how about cod, a la Lady Chatterley!'

Passing through ghost town Chunya on the way home on Sunday, we stopped by at the Mission to greet the White Fathers whom the boys had not met. We always enjoy their company and thought it might be a good lesson in how to be happy without material possessions. The Fathers were always jovial, extolling the virtues of the good life at the mission, despite its extremely Spartan frugality.

We wound them up a bit about the history of their Order in Tanganyika. I was curious about the angle the Catholic pioneers took on agricultural settlement. They told us that their Order originated in France in 1876, the first ten arriving in Bagamoyo, the slavers port of entry, in June 1878. They wore white robes which may have struck fear into the illegal slaving Arabs, for the Fathers were able to release thousands of slaves. There are records of them settling fifty to seventy thousand men and women per year. I learned that these refugee enclaves were immensely successful. How was that? The Fathers explained that the refugees had to make contributions to the mission in exchange for their security. Apparently local tribesmen also joined these de-tribalised schemes to escape the tyranny of their chiefs. The missionaries thus gained unfettered access to men's souls, something that the TANU Party aspires to today.

In modern terms I concluded that success evolved from security of land tenure, freedom from witchcraft, access to health facilities, and freedom from marauding young warrior harassment. They were willing, we were told, to work for the mission three days a week. They were also rewarded with cloth to drape their nakedness. This was when I realised that Oxfam free food would be better provided as a reward for communal work, such as roadway and village site clearing

The Fathers told us that Catholic Church attendance was mandatory on these schemes and hence conflict grew with Islam along the coastal belt. I would say that the White Fathers of yore had the Human Rights issue sorted. At Warwick School during the war we boys understood that Rights had to be earned, often the hard way.

What Jo and I came to understand as missionary mischief, in other words, the destruction of tribal culture, could be avoided at Kipembawe. However the prospect of political indoctrination could not.

After invigorating glasses of fresh lemon juice we loaded ourselves back into the Zodiac and headed for Mbeya Hills. Digesting the religion factor in development planning proved easier than digesting the smell emanating from a high sided truck holding us up on the dusty road winding through the hills. Rukwa kippers! After five miles my passengers were swooning and gasping for oxygen.

I pulled off the road and everyone collapsed on the moorland sward to breathe the cool air drifting pleasantly up and over the escarpment from Usangu 5,000 feet below us. We were at the highest point of 8,050 feet altitude, one of the highest mountain passes in the world. At this level geographers say that you can see 58 miles, but even in the rain washed atmosphere and with binoculars we could not spot any of those herds of zebra and giraffe that we chased back in December, on Bohoro Flats.

Historically cultural boundaries were delineated by consensus between tribal powers until the advent of British colonial surveyors. We inherited a concept from our Norman ancestors, namely land ownership, and legally enforceable boundaries. Supported by paper, these concepts are still new in Africa with boundaries quite unrelated to tribal or ecological factors thus leading to political strife. No-one ever forgets an imposed boundary-change, as we see today in Palestine, Ireland, Kurdistan, Kashmir, and Southern Sudan. On this occasion the problem arose because the Elton Plateau, where I am expected to plan a wheat scheme, though close to Mbeya in physical features and tribal affiliations has been surveyed into Iringa Province 240 miles away. I had therefore to drive to Iringa for discussions with Don Muir and his team.

This had a plus side for me; it meant that I could see Caroline. On this occasion I had timed it right so that I could carry her home by car at the end of term, though she was perfectly capable of looking after herself on public transport. The adventures of a fourteen year old blonde girl on a service bus in Tanganyika could be something of an unsavoury soap opera.

I headed down to the school mid-morning. I only just survived a playground pile up of giggling girls with dignity intact. I was struck amidships by a flying fourteen year old ecstatic daughter. She burst out of the dormitory doorway in a fever of excitement and took a flying leap, wrapping her legs around my waist, collapsing us in an affectionate heap. Her friends were shouting, 'Hey Caroline, who's the boyfriend?' Need I tell you how I felt about that! I was certainly moved.

She continued to effervesce throughout the 240 mile red murram dusty drive home. Her brain was in top gear and flat out, like the Zodiac, but without the punctures. She was not only full of beans, but Tommy Steele, Pythagoras, ghost stories, rock-n-roll, medieval history, Tanganyikan politics, Greek tobacco farmers problems, and the current fashion in hair style, which was, blonde and long, back and front.

I made it in forty minutes this time. No, not Iringa to Mbeya but the ubiquitous brake repair job en route; down in the mud; jack up the car; remove the wheel; strip down the brake cylinder; replace the rubbers; reassemble; and Caroline to pump the brake pedal to bleed the air out of the system with me below shouting, 'Go, stop, test, again, OK.' And off we went. Self reliance was the Gospel in our family.

It was now the height of the dry season. My Trainee, Eric Timothy, decided to get married at his remote village whilst it was still accessible by car, and I was invited as a distinguished guest, in his words. Eric was one of the up and coming generation of civil servants with a Cambridge School Certificate and destined to become a Field Officer supervising the older experienced surveyors. I was anxious that he fully appreciated the valuable work they were doing under arduous conditions and that he also learned how to do effective soil survey work in the field. Through doing this field work together we had a close and rewarding relationship. His home village was in the very far north of Chunya District.

I drove north on my own and planned to bring the bride and groom back with me to Mbeya to spend their honeymoon in the modern metropolis, an aspiration comparable with that which Jo and I had when we married at the end of the war. We left our village to revel in the culture of London for our honeymoon.

I must have hammered along 200 miles of murram road before I found my bespoke landmark to turn west into the bush. For another hour I pursued the grassy track in growing desperation, and in sweltering heat. By now I was feeling like Dr Livingstone except that the "savages" wore trousers. At the point of turning back I beheld Eric's smiling face appearing from amongst a cluster of primitive huts. It seemed like a miracle. It was certainly a relief.

When I mentioned that it seemed like a miracle, the numerous elders and religious leaders to whom I was introduced, and who all spoke English, seemed exceptionally impressed by my analogy with heavenly goodwill. I soon realised that these people were devout Moravians, a Czechoslovakian/Saxon Protestant sect that originated in Bohemia in the fifteenth century. I was unable to elucidate how, why or when these people, living in that utterly remote place, had abandoned their tribal culture in favour of this religion. Probably it had been under the rule of Deutsche Ostafrika. The old men always spoke of the Germans as the Deutsche. Apparently most of the elders were relations of Eric.

A sixteen year old girl emerged from one of the huts. She was pretty with plaited hair and western dress. I was introduced to Eric's fiancé, painfully shy at meeting her first white man. Try as I might to get her to avert her downcast eyes she would not respond. Eric played the role of the young educated, personable bridegroom with dignity and distinction, dressed in a smart suit and with his smooth command of English; he was very much of the aristocracy of the village.

The celebrations were in full swing and several rings of people were dancing in circles in the dust. I noticed that this was not the usual tribal exposition but inhibitive religious choral music. The order of day was jiving to church music only, and no drinking or joking. Never the less jubilation prevailed. I sat and chatted with a man they all called Babu, which is Swahili for grandfather. Some of the men were very old, they could not even say when they were born, but they could remember being adults in the First War. I often had to question the accepted statistic for life expectancy of 45 years for Africans. These old men were all straight backed and mobile, with full sets of teeth, despite never having heard of the word dentist, or was it because of that?

No doubt the isolation of these people was instrumental in maintaining their social strengths, for they were industrious, happy, crime free, witchcraft and political influence free.

I ate the village food and slept in my own mud hut, private except for the scurrying cockroaches and a helpful hungry cockerel. Sunday was the third day of celebrations. The Moravians were significantly clean and well dressed, extremely polite, waiting upon my every need. Eric's fiancé eventually revealed her large saucer dark eyes to me and I was finding her endearingly shy look quite appealing. I gathered that it was customary for aspirant brides to bow their heads and adopt a shy manner. On this Sunday she had her head covered for the wedding ceremony.

This area was lower than Kipembawe and very much hotter, were it not for my black umbrella I would have suffered heat stroke sitting in the open, for the church had no roof. The church was otherwise laid out like any church in England with me occupying an embarrassing seat of honour, like the Archbishop of Canterbury, on the raised alter dais, dressed in shorts and sporting my London umbrella like a proverbial cannibal chief.

I was subsequently photographed for posterity with the full wedding group, and once the veil was off I took a picture of the happy bride, and one of Eric regally sporting a most genial smile and a new fancy walking stick to affirm his now elevated status in the community.

As soon as the camera's eye was removed, so was the bride! To my surprise she was not yet his. Old African custom now prevailed over religion. The bride was confined to her family, in a hut opposite Eric's, and his efforts to enter being firmly rebuffed in favour of barter between Eric's brothers and the in-laws. He was obliged to pay for his nuptial fulfilment. The money offered was referred to as recompense for the loss of their hard working daughter's contribution to the welfare of the elderly members of her family. Envoys passed from hut to hut for hours, from groom to mother in-law; an auction lasting the day long and leaving Eric in considerable debt. He would not be able to fulfil his debt by working in the in-laws' fields, as is customary, so it had to be some cash on the nail plus a percentage from his salary to follow.

Two years later I called upon the couple in their government quarters. Exactly nine months after the wedding they had had twins. Of the shy village girl there was no trace. Mrs Timothy was now the dominating personality in the house, 'Can I offer you tea Mr Dawtrey?'

By August 1963, after many weeks spent under canvass in the exclusive company of Africans, giraffes, and tsetse flies, traversing a massive survey grid on foot, sampling soils to a depth of three feet, I was in a position to demonstrate on paper that those deep granitic tobacco sands were very extensive all over the Kipembawe area. The potential was obviously substantial for the production of exportable Virginia tobacco, even on the scale of Northern Rhodesia. But would those doubting-thomases in Dar be convinced?

Chapter Twelve

800 Miles Back to School and those Elephants

It was the boys' end of term but on this occasion not our happiest day. They came bounding in euphorically declaring, 'Yippee ... Mom ... no more school ... the government's closing it down to white boys!'

We did not exactly match the boys' jubilation at this disastrous news, in fact we were stunned into stony silence. The boys sensed they were on perilous ground and fell silently apprehensive. The open window heralded a coarse caw from the garden ravens which echoed our mood. I glanced at Jo, her face told all, she was heart broken and slowly melted into tears. She's a tough resourceful lady but at times frustration simply overwhelms her. The two farmer's sons, of course, did not immediately appreciate the implications. For them it was victory for common sense over pointless time-wasting academy.

I could sense that Jo was on the verge of saying, albeit unwillingly, 'Now we'll have to go back the England.' She refrained, 'Now what? The only other school open to white boys is Arusha, 800 miles away.' Even Sally sensed the despair and looked glum, ears down, eyes showing the whites as though she had committed some great offence of non-compliance. Jo continued, 'Boarding school. Philip is only eight and a half! Are we supposed to sacrifice our emotional stability for African political stability?'

I had yet to tell her that I had received a letter that day from St Michael's and St George's in Iringa to say that the government was closing Caroline's school to white children also, in December. Our innate goodwill towards our black brethren began to ebb away. The boundary line between nationalism and racialism was looking frail indeed. We were helpless. We decided to make the most of this school holiday with the children.

We were not allowed to brood for long, 'Dad! Some rotten shamba boy has diverted our water furrow at the top of the hill.' As if we didn't have enough problems our vegetable supply was now threatened. 'OK? Can Phil, Sally and me go on a dam busting raid, Dad?'

'You want me to condone trespass? No such thing in this country. Off you go. For goodness sake keep out of sight.'

I pretended not to notice the face painting with soot from the Tanganyika boiler and their departure through a hole in the high hedge with a black spaniel on a tight lead. They were gone for hours, but appeared at the lunch table with cherubic white faces and a grinning Samson in waiting. I looked through the window; Sally was lapping at the furrow.

On Monday I received a message from the Regional Game Warden's office inviting me round for a chat. David Ansty said, 'There are three factors that precipitated this interview; one, you are a bush-wise officer moving in remote areas. Two, you are staying on when so many expatriates are leaving. Three, I gather you are skilled in the conservation of soil and water and I've learned that you want to include wildlife. Am I right so far?'

'Absolutely!'

'So, on behalf of the government I'm offering you the honorary appointment of Game Warden. What do you say Brian?'

'I am most grateful for the opportunity. As a matter of fact I did write to Mervyn Cowie years ago seeking a job in the Kenya National Parks and of course he said that I'd need to get African experience first.'

'Oh. I know Mervyn very well. The government has agreed to designate Bohoro Flats, down on Usangu as a Controlled Hunting Area and I need help there too. I know for a fact that those Texan missionaries from Chimala have been down there with shot guns and motor bikes shooting at lions. Any chance of you getting down that way?'

'Jo and I have a plan to drive across there and reach Iringa. I'm not sure when though. Any way I can do a week-end safari when I get a word from Japanese de Villiers that something's going on.'

'I don't trust de Villiers. Any way that's up to you. Here's your ID card and your name will be in the Government Gazette next month.'

The news was a boost to us all at home. The boys really hoped that we'd all end up living in a National Park.

Unfortunately, concurrent with this news I received a message from our Iringa friends the Mansfields to say that Hilda had died, apparently from an injury received on safari. They both went on safari together a lot. She received an injury that became gangrenous and the Iringa hospital could not cope with it adequately. They put her on the bus to Dar es Salaam, 316 miles, and she died after surgery in Dar hospital. We shall sadly miss their lovely stories. Jo stoically declared that she would still accompany me on safari. Thank goodness.

The next RDC was a typical African assembly. It was dynamic forum for which Africans have great talent, hugely time consuming and patience-demanding for a European. I was seated by 8.30 am, but no sign of the Chairman. This was how the meeting proceeded:

At 9.45 am the Chairman sweeps in briskly, gasping that he was rushed off his feet and profusely apologetic for being late. He is accompanied by several confidantes, all full of bonhomie and aplomb. The chairman is followed by the main body of African members, who pour into the hall in a hubbub of enthusiasm, triggered off by some secret knowledge that the much loved Minutes, are about to be read. It is now 10.15 am, time for the usual magnificent rendering of the National Anthem. Two hours later the minutes are adopted, with numerous amendments. Then, low and behold, the missing member arrives and after a lengthy diatribe on the subject of unavoidable delays on important business, he requests to be brought up to date on proceedings so far. This takes some time! It is now 11.0 am and the Agenda can begin.

On this occasion I was advised by the chairman who was also the Regional Commissioner, Waziri Juma, that I was required to conduct an official guest of the Government to Kipembawe to review The Plan. I was to understand that he was a top level German Agricultural Economic Advisor to the Tanganyika Government.

Such meetings tended to be, not only the beginning of new aspirations, but also the end of everything. Oratory seems to be a genetic link to black skin colour. Resolutions were the ultimate in attainment. Implementation, however, was something that could be left to expatriates, who were considered to be able to stick their necks out without fear of political or ancestral spiritual recrimination. Any commitment, I had yet to learn, from an individual African, was totally valueless unless backed by his whole peer group. He would fall at the first fence. The only chance of progress was full RDC support for every single move. To achieve that I made my presentiments in such a way that the whole idea appeared in the Minutes as their idea. It was quite heavy going.

On the occasion of this Rural Development meeting there was lengthy debate as to whether convicted women prisoners should receive lashes the same as men. There was general agreement that they should. They had, however, no authority at all in the matter. After more lengthy discussion it was finally decided that it was nothing to do with rural development, which was quite a relief.

The Vice-President later condemned our resolution. He also decreed that the punishment for theft would be henceforth a minimum of two years imprisonment; whilst for cattle rustling, seven years would be reduced to three, but with lashes administered quarterly. Corporal punishment was increased to 24 lashes per year. The inherent pattern of British justice was changing complexion.

Usangu week-end: Second to Lake Rukwa, talk of Usangu always aroused whoops of joy. When Jean and Eric came round with a suggestion for the week-end, there was no need to await a response. To reach the Bohoro Flats we had to cross a river bed. Water was still flowing so it was off-fan belts for wading plus pushers behind. Unfortunately when the bonnet rose up the bank opposite, the boot dropped under the water behind and soaked our bread. We placed it on the roof rack to dry in the sun.

We made camp towards dusk, Jean enquired, 'anyone know any bed time stories?'

'Yes I do.' I said stepping in where angels feared to. 'This is true. A few years ago there was a family of lions hereabouts. The mother lion taught her cubs to be fearless, even when there were humans near. When they grew up they took a fancy to human meat, which is very unusual after all, and they killed more than a thousand people over the years, between here and Njombe.'

'I did suggest a bed-time story!'

'These lions used to rush into a herd of cattle and not touch the cows but take the herd boy. A famous Mbeya game warden named George Rushby was called in and he avowed to kill all the lions. Weeks turned into months without his bullets finding their mark. The lions were just too clever, never striking at the same place twice. The villagers decided that the lions must be immortal, re-incarnated ancestral spirits, and all became fatalistic, resulting in George Rushby losing their support completely. He was a determined hunter however and eventually he shot them all. They were the most enormous beasts with heads as big a bubble car. By that time they had killed nearly one thousand people. I can assure you all, as an Honorary Game Warden myself, that there has been no report of man-eating lions since then. You may hear distant lions roaring at night but you can go to bed without fear of them, their roar carries for miles.'

The silence was disturbed only by the crackle of sticks on the fire as a breeze caught it. Jean braced herself. 'Hmm, I've only got one comment to make about that bed time story. One of us will need to be kipping by the fire with his rifle. And that person will be ... need I say'

That night in my bed by the fire I enjoyed the company of Sally Spaniel and Buster Spaniel, an exciting couple, but only in the daytime. Buster deserted me when the fire died down and the clear sky drew the heat out of it. He sloped off to the tent for warmth amongst the snoring bodies.

Suddenly there was a protracted scream from the tent followed by general panic. Dazed children rolled off their camp beds and stood up. Soon the flashing torches under the canvass went out and calm returned. Apparently Buster had licked a somnolent face, much as a lion might lick the flesh off the bone of its victim.

My only recollection of the night life was the chill of dawn and a bursting bladder, which forced me out of my bag into the secrecy of a thorn bush. Adding to the hostility of the two inch thorns, a squadron of thirsty fire ants arrived to avail themselves of the fountain from heaven. I escaped just in time to find that during my absence from the camp fire an ember had settled on my sleeping bag and converted it to a charred mass. The breeze had fanned the flames and a snowstorm of feathers drifted across the camp site. It was barely light, a bleary eyed Jean appeared. 'It's snowing, get up folks! Our white hunter's done it again. He's magic this man.'

I blushingly enjoyed the open air fried bacon, tomatoes and eggs 'charmingly served', I observed. 'Flattery, will get you no further than the washing up bowl Bwana Nyama.' (Game Warden)

We didn't find any poachers on Bohoro Flats but we had a wonderful safari week-end prior to the dreaded start of another school term.

A day of desolation hit us after the departure of our two boys on the service bus to their new school in Arusha 800 miles away. We have never been so distraught in our lives over anything. The bus had a first class compartment at the front into which all the white children from Mbeya were seated, separated from the heaving mass of travellers and chickens behind. The three day safari was going to take guts. Parents too would be in limbo for news, for seven days, because of communication problems.

News came through sooner than we expected, the proverb "no news is good news," was born out on this occasion. There was a message in my office from Italian parent Mr Sossi, "Children's bus hit a bank and overturned. Will call and pick you up, Sossi."

Parents gathered at our house to meet a trembling Mr Sossi as he spoke through his moustache, 'I tink de children OK. Better we follow Mr Dawtrey and one of us can take de children on to Iringa and de udder to come back wid de news. What you say?'

'OK Mr Sossi, let's go.'

We found the bus 40 miles out, on its side. The African passengers and the driver were nowhere to be seen. The roof of the bus was all bubbly where passengers' heads had struck. A small group of white children, dressed in their green uniforms and grey hats, huddled in the shade of a nearby tree, apparently none the worse for their experience. Richard was the eldest, 'I took them all out through the front windscreen, across the engine. No-one's hurt. We've been waiting hours Dad. Can you get us to Iringa in time for the second school bus?' Here we have a potential leader, I thought.

'Yes. Sorry about all this Richard, you've done well caring so well for all these children. Congratulations. We'll just have a quick look at what caused the crash, shall we.' The brazing that held the steering track rod end inside its socket on this old Albion bus had failed and pulled out.

Some weeks later we received a parcel from the school, it contained shredded clothes. Apparently the children had picked up acid from the battery under the drivers seat as they climbed out through the front windscreen.

At least Jo was now free to accompany me to Matwiga. I needed to continue my soil survey work, procuring soil samples for Tengeru Research Station. I was soon dreaming, "sandy clay, clay loam, sandy clay loam, weak structure, moderately weak structure, colour 7.5YR, (which is yellow), 2.5 YR (which is red), dendritic, organic, fauna; evidence of termites" etc etc. This last section on fauna took an unexpectedly dramatic turn one day.

Life in camp after a hot day sampling soils and tramping miles was as ever a joy, bathing together in the cool crystal clear deep water of the Mkowiji stream, whilst our African surveyors too splashed riotously at a discreet distance, totally unabashed by their nakedness. In the cool of the evening Jo and I relaxed beside the camp fire listening to ever popular stories of hunting dangerous animals, and of ancient tribal rituals and superstitions. Since my staff were of various unrelated tribes from far off corners of Tanganyika, with tribal histories going back to the 17th century, there was much of interest to everyone.

132

Alexander Maki was a most likeable mature man with an unusually coal black shiny skin, indicating his ancient origins from the Congo via his Lake Victoria Wasukuma tribe. Despite his dignified manner, he always had a knowing mischievous twinkle in his eye, and loved a joke, as did Jo of course! Charades provided a natural stage for her too and the camp revelled in it. Miming Professor Pima again, this time with the Memsa-b's reactions, adding spice to ever popular satire.

Encounters with elephants were like encounters with Maasai, one felt that the landscape was theirs, by right of occupation since creation, and that one was an intruder upon a primordial society, with Rights. In the early morning of our 'elephant day' Jo and I headed off into the endless monotony of dusty miombo woodland in search of the latest soil pits dug for me. This time I was accompanied by my "bush secretary", as Alexander called Jo. I carried a satchel of 'goodies' for work, and survival in remote corners of nowhere, whilst Jo clutched a clip board and my brass ringed black London umbrella, 'for defence against the sun, and those lions,' that we had encountered unpleasantly before in Matwiga.

Hiking through the sunny silent woods alone, might sound romantic and in fact we were reminded of our teenage years during the war when Jo and I strolled hand in hand in the cool fresh verdant woods of Leek Wootton in Warwickshire, listening to the echo of rattling woodpeckers and crowing cock pheasants.

How we yearned for those cool Warwickshire woods on our 'elephant day'. It was so hot and ominously silent, there was an air of lurking danger, and then that manic call began, of African 'rain bird', a type of cuckoo which has a monotonous incessant call of three descending notes. It just never stops, driving us close to insanity by the day's end. Like the sneaky, evil English cuckoo this little Emerald Spotted version is rarely seen but incessantly heard.

Soil profile inspection pits are neatly cut six feet deep and six feet long, by three feet wide. Ominous did you say? I have survived many happy hours below ground level, seeking to understand what happened to the landscape 100,000 years ago, and how its nutrient status might have been affected today. I collected my soil samples in small cotton bags. It was a long thirsty process, relieved only by Jo's presence, sitting above me like an angel in the sky, "taking down".

A tranquil hour passed in the shade of the umbrella. 'Brian! Do you hear that rumbling sound? I think I know what it might be.'

We pensively listened. There was a valley bottom mbuga nearby with a stream running through it. Straining our eyes we could just make out amongst the trees, a herd of elephants ambling along towards us. Our scent was sliding down the slope towards them and I gauged our situation to be dicey. The old matriarch was already signalling to the rest of her tribe to 'up trunks' and take the air. One could almost hear her thinking 'human smell here, better take a closer sniff.'

She approached through the trees as nimbly as a ballet dancer. 'Quick Brian, lets get out of here. They're coming.'

The matriarch sent extra sensory alarm signals through to her family back in the mbuga resulting in a frightening turmoil of uncertainty, rising dust and cries of fear amongst the juniors in the herd. Two more 'heavies' joined in the rush towards us, their trunks raised like tea-pot spouts, trying to pin-point the source of our 'obnoxious' aroma.

Jo with all serenity said, 'Well Professor, have you decided what to do yet!' and then in panic mode, 'Here they come. Make room for me.'

She leaped down beside me and we curled up in the bottom like two woodlice beneath the half open black umbrella. This was not the first tight corner we'd been in. *'Could be our last,'* I thought, *'at least we'll be buried together.'*

'They're a lively bunch aren't they.' Came a trembling whisper from Jo. 'Not like those posers in the movies.'

Suddenly we were showered with sand from shuffling heavy feet above us. 'She smells the blood of an Englishman.' I foolishly muttered as we cling together like Hansel and Gretel. 'Hope they can't go down on their knobbly knees. Have you ever heard of an elephant with its head stuck in a hole?'

'Idiot!'

A mountain of crinkly grey skin loomed above us, blocking the light out for a second, then moved away to be replaced by another. We both cringed beneath the brolly trying to be invisible, more soil showered down. I thought, *'Glad they've got poor eye sight.'* Suddenly something of a more noxious nature dropped into Jo's lap in a steaming barrowful, pinning her down. I slammed my grubby hand across her mouth to prevent any startled comment. We were both gasping in ammonia fumes.

Suddenly it was quiet. We are alone again, surviving, as ever, just the two of us, and our compost from heaven. 'OK we've been in a midden before.' I confidently declared, 'Let's see what's going on.'

I tentatively peeped over the edge of the soil pit; nothing. 'They've gone.' I looked down at Jo, she sat slumped in the corner of the pit, hair all ruffled, hat cock-eyed, trembling with relief, nursing her compost. A tear rolled. 'Just look at my trousers!'

'Sorry. Tell you what, wash them in the stream and I'll hang them up in the tree to dry in the sun. We can finish the pit, you can keep your knickers on. Go on, make my day.'

In typical British style we finished the pit, against all the odds.

'It must have been the dung balls that saved us, disguising our scent. Heaven sent you might say! Then again you might not.'

With Jo now in her knickers I ventured a smile and wrote on her soil pit description sheet under "fauna", "elephant indications." I recalled a camp fire story about a Game Scout who had a similar experience to us; he fell in tall grass when retreating from a charging elephant. The Game Scout said, 'Tembo couldn't see me I was so close, in fact it was actually standing over me. In a frenzy of fear tembo suddenly felt the need, like me and peed all over me. I took the full blast, it was like Victoria Falls, and I couldn't even gasp in the deluge. But it saved my life.'

After a while our survey Land Rover came winding its way through the trees towards us. The driver must have seen Jo struggling into her clammy pants. 'Jambo Bwana na Memsa-b. Solly to interlupt. Thought me heard tembo. Any ploblem with tembo Bwana?'

'Ha-ku-na!' I reply nonchalantly, meaning 'of course not! 'You've come to save us then Okera? You're a bit late! They've been and gone. They came to look in our soil pit. I talked with the Big One. She said "Looks good for tobacco Bwana. If you want any trees removed we can do it for you Bwana." I told the Big One, "When we're ready we'll send Okera Mwakajinga to you with a message".'

Peels of laughter from under the canopy and murmurings in Swahili, 'Bwana mganga iko.' Bwana is witchdoctor.

At the end of the soil pits job, when preparing for the 150 mile run back to Mbeya, I broke my Ford Zodiac front cross member on a tree stump. We feared that our stay might be prolonged and lead to 'famine in the camp'. The village labourers were brilliant with their bark rope - wet and dry. They managed to strap the iron like a splint and we set off, fingers crossed, for Mbeya. Fortunately it had rained across the Mbeya mountain passes which softened the road and tightened the bark string.

Back at Mbeya Golf Club that week-end, Jo related, over her gin and tonic, her version of events, with a twist in the tale, 'I lost my trousers while fleeing in the bush and was holed-in-one by an elephant.'

Chapter Thirteen

The Messerschmit Pilot and Elton Plateau

I collected the elderly Dr G., whom I shall refrain from naming fully, from the airport and brought him home to meet the Regional Commissioner Waziri Juma, at our house. Jo had prepared an excellent lunch. Dr G. had obviously been briefed to look at Kipembawe area, and he wanted to do it all in one day, I felt on sufferance? I explained that it was 320 miles round trip on murram roads, but he was determined to convince us that he was not deterred by such trifles.

His conversation began to get irksomely pompous and, over coffee, he over-stepped the mark by boasting about his achievements as a Messerschmitt pilot during the war and retrospectively prophesying that, 'we could easily have won the war if Hitler had not made the fatal mistake of turning to attack Russia instead of Britain, on September 15th 1940.'

I felt I should moderate the tenor of his claim, 'I recall that date very well because we won the air battle then with our Spitfires. 80 German planes a day were being shot down. It was that that decided Adolf to change tactics and invade Russia. There was another contributory factor don't forget, 'Bulldog' Churchill was awaiting him on that little island across the Channel. Hitler recognised Churchill as just as uncompromising and dangerous as himself.'

Waziri Juma was wreathed in smiles over this minor skirmish. He had been educated in England. Doctor G. then sought sympathy by telling us that he had suffered a broken neck during the conflict. At which point I decided to make the journey in our survey Land Rover instead of my car.

I rolled out the 'red carpet' for my guest, it was dusty and corrugated, commonly known as murram. His voice warbled endlessly during the journey, shouting above the noise of the engine running flat out from dawn until dusk as Okera kept his foot flat on the boards.

He shouted. 'Luftwaffe pilots hated the rash, casual confidence of British pilots in the face of the German chivalrous professional pilots, they were lambs to the slaughter.'

I was sorely tempted to retaliate with my personal experience of German chivalry; us boys were machine gunned on the playing fields at Coventry Grammar School. However I restrained myself for the sake of Matwiga settlers.

The shameless Dr G. pursued his vendetta, 'Germany would have conquered the whole world, once we'd gained control of the British Empire. We wouldn't have tolerated this Independence nonsense. Tanganyika would have been developed into a prosperous nation by now.'

At this point we swept through flames from the burning forest, which somehow seemed appropriate to the conversation. But his beard was not singed, 'We would have stopped all this bush burning too, destroying all the organic matter that is needed to enrich the soil. We would have made the blacks obey, with a taste of the kiboko. Look what they have achieved in South Africa with a bit of discipline.'

Glances were exchanged with my driver Okera, who understood English, after which the doctor fell silent for a bit.

On the way home after dark he began to complain bitterly of the pain in his neck, from his war wound. There was a false cough from Okera, and I smiled in the dark. I remembered my own shrapnel wounds from the Coventry Blitz. It was these wounds that fortuitously put me into a hospital where I met a young St John's Ambulance Brigade cadet named Cicely May; later to be nick named Jo. I have to thank Adolf for that. He would turn in his grave if he knew what happiness he had created.

Dr G.'s official report recommended an expatriate manager for Matwiga Scheme. I have to thank him for that wise judgment; it was just what I needed. He did not recommend an infusion of capital however; he knew the cupboard was bare.

The build up of black thunder clouds over Mbeya heralded the start of the rains and planting time. Recruiting of Wenela Repatriates for Matwiga began in earnest, in Tukuyu. There were already 3,000 applicants mostly young married men, ex. RSA gold mines. Selecting the right sort of men to pioneer what would be a tough assignment needed a wise selection team. It was lead by Bob Silcock, backed up with my Senior Surveyor Alexander Maki, the Chunya District Agricultural Officer Ramus Lyatuu, the African District Secretary and Tim Smith our VSO. What a good team!

Oxfam have begun to move American World Food Programme, WFP, maize, milk powder, cooking oil and nutritional biscuits to Matwiga, where my surveyors' labourers had cleared a reception area in the forest. It had taken me 16 months to get this far against stiff Ministry disdain. A good expatriate manager was expected to report to us any day. I could now give more attention to the Elton Plateau.

Opportunity-knocked for Jo and me and off we went again together, this time to a log cabin in the uninhabited high mountains of the tribal kingdom of Uwanji. On the way we stopped to hobnob with the chief, Jumbe Solomon, at his village called Matamba, on a lower plateau. His kingdom topped two giant sized steps, the first a 3,000 ft vertical climb up a winding track of 54 hair-pin bends from Usangu rift valley to first plateau, and the second 2,500 ft from Matamba to the wilderness of Elton Plateau at about 8,500 ft altitude, with volcanic crags reaching 9,715 ft. It was a freezing cold place at night. We had a primus stove with us to keep warm, as the area is totally treeless.

Solomon told Jo that no African had ever slept in the mountains and survived. He said that the high plateau was inhabited by Wawanji ancestral spirits, also leopards. Apparently the former could enter the minds of the latter and visit Wawanji villages in order to kill anyone that had been accused of witchcraft, or adultery. or robbery. 'No need of policemen here!' declared the chief with aplomb.

'Brian has slept up there many times,' Jo told him with tongue in cheek, 'with those ancestral spirits of yours pounding upon his cabin door. He doesn't look too bad on it does he? '

'The Bwana's ancestral spirits are obviously more powerful than ours.' Solomon looked serious. 'Bwana. Now that you are taking your wife to stay up there, remember what I told you before. Men's minds, and for that matter women, can fall under the influence of spiritual forces. They hold sway up there in that terrible place. You notice that your surveyors will never stay overnight up there. They are wise.

Kitulo is the Uwanji tribal name for what the Victorians decreed should be called Elton Plateau, after the explorer who 'discovered' it. Cotterell, one of Captain James Elton's Party, kept the journey log, a copy of which I had procured from the Royal Geographical Society, of which I am a Fellow.

Cotterell indicated that they crossed the plateau in two hours walking non-stop and made no comment other than it was like Switzerland, and uninhabited. This epitaph to his later demise as a result of crossing Usangu, seemed to me most inappropriate. I had shown Solomon the log. Solomon had never heard of Elton.

'Now Bwana... I have pleasure in telling you that I and my tribal elders have agreed to relinquish 30,000 acres of Kitulo land to the Tanganyika Government, for your United Nations Wool Sheep Scheme.'

'That's wonderful news Solomon, I'm overjoyed. Your people will praise you for it in the long run, of that I am sure.'

N.B. Kitulo later became a National Park.

Jumbe Solomon invited us to his ngoma to celebrate the occasion. We accepted.

An African ngoma is an anything-goes sort of booze up/crazy dance/sexual orgy. Jo and I stayed overnight at the Matamba government rest house, i.e., four brick walls, a tin roof and a drop pit choo under the stars. Unusually there was a chimney so we collected wood from the escarpment and made a fire. In preparation for the ngoma I pulled up my long white socks, secured them with my somewhat perished garters and stood before Jo in my sparkling white colonial shorts and shirt hoping for admiration. 'Good looking chap? Legs a bit spindly. I must get some thicker socks when we go on leave.'

The ngoma was in full swing when we arrived. Jo wore her slacks for the cool night air and I shone like a pearl in the half light of the fire. The dancing was led by the tribal mganga, frighteningly bedecked in white paint, feathers, ankle bells, strings of crocodile teeth, and strips of leopard skin covering his 'possible'. The 'live music' consisted of a group of men dressed in torn vests and ragged trousers, chanting mournfully on bamboo pipes. By blowing across the tops of the hollow bamboos of various thicknesses, different see-sawing notes in a minor key emerged, to waft across the cool mountain air. These eerie sounds were pounded into a rhythm by a very corpulent drum. An occasional relief for the drummer was provided by the mee-owing of a one string viola that really turned our stomachs.

At first I did not hesitate to get amongst the bouncing brown breasts, jangling beads and shining black eyes. The incessantly see-sawing 'music' crept into my psyche; my pombe laden blood stream conveyed the pounding rhythm to my brain, so that everything seemed a lot more real than reality; gigantic black nipples, devouringly large lips and sharp teeth.

Many of the girls had their teeth sharpened to points, like sharks, which they considered the height of beauty, though I found them rather intimidating in the half light. Soon the girls got into a frenzied trance state and I beat a hasty retreat to a chair next to Solomon and Jo. Jo wasn't really into this kind of madness, she was taking a more circumspect view of the whole proceedings, including the imbibing of communal buckets of cardboard tasting pombe.

The pombe speaking through me recounted to Solomon what a French girl once said to me. 'Sophisticated Parisien women say that breasts should be secreted away for the enjoyment of their men folk.'

Solomon looked blank. It had never occurred to him that there could be anything pleasurable about breasts. Now pointed teeth! He thought that was sexy.

The acrid smelling mganga appeared and we stood up to greet him. Solomon interpreted. He spoke over our heads, with imperious authority on the subject of Brian Dawtrey and his destiny, expressing scepticism about the scheme for wool sheep. 'There are chui up there you know,' meaning leopards; nodding towards the mountains, 'they'll eat the your nyama,' meaning the imported wool sheep, 'Our ancestors will reincarnate into Chui and become the heralds of death. They'll come down here and wreak vengeance upon us all for giving our land to the government.'

'You think our lives are in danger then?' I asked pointedly.

Mganga fixed me with a penetrating gaze and a pointing a finger saying, 'Bwana, if...' Solomon broke in concernedly, 'No no Bwana, of course not. We know that your efforts will bring great benefits to my people, and I am sure that you will be in favour with our ancestors. I predict that you will be rewarded pleasurably while you are up there with your wife working in that terrible place.'

Mganga turned briskly and marched off.

Up on the high plateau downland next day, we encountered a risky deep gully crossing over rustic loose timber decking which the ever resourceful Jo crocheted into a stable platform. After several miles of spectacularly floriferous rolling landscape we reached the log cabin, built by Forest Department. It lay deep down in a valley with the Mtorwi 9,715 foot rocky peak towering above like the Matterhorn in a mini Switzerland of floral slopes. It was uncannily quiet in the cabin at night but for the sound of tumbling Mkowiji stream past the door.

The next day Jo and I strode over the downlands of that wild place in the sky. The utter silence was broken only by the plaintive cries of eagles swirling on the thermals above us and the occasional far away cow bell. We were alone again, as we had been on that 'elephant day' in Matwiga. Would there be any nasty surprises here? No elephants at this altitude.

We wandered on, ankle deep in flowers of an hundred rare species, created with the plateau before Man. There were courtship displays of small birds, and migrants passing high over head to warmer southern climes. 'What's that over there Brian looks like a huge black hovering butterfly.'

'Oh, that's the male widow bird. It dangles its long black tail and flashes its red wing feathers whilst hovering over its mate in the grass below. Here, take the binoculars, you'll see her there, pretending to ignore his antics. The girls eventually fall for it "hook, line, and sinker". Do you think if I wave my arms frantically, with my shorts round my knees, I would make a more impressive suitor?'

'I can say from first hand knowledge ... that it depends upon whether you are facing north or south.'

Despite the beauty of Kitulo we felt an air of unearthly isolation, a wild timelessness that provoked the unknown depths of the psyche. We were cautious when jumping across streams in the valleys in case of a leopard crouching there amongst the tree heather. No man has ever survived leopard attack.

This rain soaked plateau, guarded by leopards and Wawanji spirits, is mantled with wind blown pumiceous ash from Rungwe volcano that retains the water like a sponge in the sky. This sponge feeds the Great Ruaha and Rufiji Rivers that nourish the whole of Southern Tanganyika. He who ventures to plough it will put the nation in peril.

Further to the east along the Kipengere Range the land drops enough in altitude to accommodate a tribe called Wakinga. In the Njombe District Office I had earlier found Field Reports for 1939 by D.O. Craig Macdonald. He recorded that people used to live in holes in the ground during the frosty season, and that women were naked except for a bunch of leaves, collected fresh each morning, and the men nothing at all. The latter he says were usually befuddled with bamboo wine. He monitored 50 women over his very long tour of duty and recorded the birth of 300 babies, of which only 70 survived.

The Iringa Department of Water Affairs produced a Plan to draw water from Ukinga and channel it from the mountains to the rainless plains of Usangu below by means of a simple concrete catchment device. This had been placed where a stream goes over the on the edge of the escarpment. I had been told that it was already installed on trial. The old tribal enmities however had emerged and there was opposition to the notion of the mountain people providing their historical enemies below with life giving water.

Angus, a wild haired Scottish Highlander was the water engineer and two other expatriate engineers and their wives, were to be our guests on the plateau. We met them down in Matamba. The cabin was too small for everybody. It was decided that the four wives should go down below the mountains to the abandoned Igawa Ranch house. This old colonial sprawling house was quite romantic, with its wide spacious views of the mountains, well kept lawns and banana plants bordering a cool stream. The old place was still fully furnished, with its echoes of hunting parties, and wife swapping parties while the servants barbecued an ox on the lawn. The walls were festooned with trophy heads of huge buffalo with spreading black horns and glassy eyes glaring down revengefully through the cobwebs. The evenings could be spooky by paraffin lamps and bats emerging to seek moths that had pupated in the trophy heads. We men folk intended to be back there before dark.

I conducted the engineers to that remote corner of the Ukinga mountains, where the experimental catchment device was. Could it survive the coming rainy season? Angus seemed quite at home in the hills. The air was cool and clammy with soft clouds creeping about the hills around us at ground level. I was glad to park my bare knees near the gear box in their Land Rover. We rode it like a horse for miles over eroded tracks. When we stopped the silence was bewildering. One forgets what real silence is like.

Finally we had to trek, for half a mile to the edge of the precipitous escarpment. The trap had become blocked by fallen rocks and everyone set-to to lift them clear. 'You know Brian,' said Angus quietly, as though respecting the silence of the place, 'the chiefs of Usangu and Ukinga have agreed to this scheme, but I reckon that there could still be a sabotage element by young hooligans from the Ukinga tribe who haven't been consulted.'

We gazed around us, somewhat fearfully, at the green rising hilly slopes surrounding us, feeling that we might be under observation by tribesmen, or spiritual forces? Then Andrew said loudly 'Hey! Look there, a figure, standing high up on that crag. Do you see?'

We only glimpsed the figure before it disappeared. We returned to our deliberations feeling that it was just a traveller from Lake Malawi passing through. Woolly clouds seem to be chasing each other across the ridges behind us in increasing numbers. One of them rolled across a shoulder of grassland behind us revealing three near naked black men. Suddenly they came prancing down the slope, yelling and waving cutlasses and spears.

I now saw that their small spears had barbed shafts to prevent them from falling out of their victims bodies. They had painted their faces white, doubtless to invoke the more powerful white man's spirits to support them. On their heads, they wore long haired black Colobus monkey skins, looking like guardsmen's busbies. They looked formidable. They obviously meant business. Their white striped nakedness, ubiquitous talismans, not to mention elephantine swinging genitals, completed a picture of rash false bravado, which offered no prospect of negotiation. The challenge was clear and uncompromising; it was kill or be killed. There were three of them and four of us, and whether we were right or wrong in our enterprise became of secondary importance to our survival.

I always carried my Maasai simi on safari, thank goodness. This murderous long bladed cutlass was sharpened on both edges and weighted towards the point. I drew my simi threateningly.

Angus, heightened by his highland instincts of retaliation, had managed to wrench the spear off the one assailant and in a red faced fury threw it at the retreating couple. Was this really what overseas aid was all about?

We were more evenly matched now, and the two African warriors reeling with surprise, give us a few seconds to decide tactics. We decided to jump on one warrior and disarm him, then threaten the third. This trick worked and no African blood was spilt on Ukinga soil.

Angus was now shouting at me to grab the haversack and bolt. Across the valley I reached the Land Rover and look back at the horrific scene below. Undoubtedly disadvantaged by dagaa, African hashish, our assailants had lost their nerve but still adopted a threatening pose. Angus, backed by his two colleagues, was shouting angrily and bounding uphill after them like Rob Roy.

Trembling and in shock, adrenaline running high, we decided upon a morale booster before going to report to the boma in far away Njombe. We headed off for 'the girls' down at the ranch. I tried to be a cheery host, 'what say we run the girls naked round the ranch then?' uncertain whether my illustrious companions were quite as bush-hardened as me.

'Great! That sounds magnificent.' Said Andrew, the retiring English gentleman with a curly moustache and a torn safari jacket, 'I'm just in the mood for a bit of rumpy pumpy, after that battle.'

The others tremblingly grinned and said nowt for the next hour.

"Back at the ranch" the 'girls' were out walking in the hot sun light. 'Let's round 'em up,' spurted Andrew obviously feeling a bit wild-west-ish.

We huddled together on the veranda and explained the dreadful events of the day, of how we went in search of water and instead we found warriors.

'God .... That's terrible. I'm amazed how perky you all look.' said wide eyed Janet, 'what's happened to put smiles on your faces then?'

'Well, we did win, and we've got a plan, to assert our new found warrior status!' That was Andrew with a glint in his eye. That man's nature under stress was a revelation.

'Oh!' responds Janet, 'if it's a booze-up you want, we can offer you stream water, flavoured with cows hooves.'

'First of all, the warriors are going to strip naked in the mountain stream, wash, and then we're all yours. They say that Africa is dynamic, a land of horrors, and ecstasies. We've had the horrors and now it's time for the ecstasies. How about you girls joining us in the stream?' Andrew was really getting into his stride, filling the rest of us with consternation.

With gasps of derision, and blushes, Janet glanced at the other wives and softly conceded with a sly titter, 'OK .... We'll join you warriors in a mo.'

'Brian!' confided Jo, 'are you sure about this? No cross pollination mind.'

'If anyone else comes for you I'll draw my simi and shorten 'im up a bit.'

Certain boldness emerged amongst the engineers' wives; I suppose they wouldn't be here at all if they weren't bold by nature. The warriors seemed shy to expose their weapons at first and dashed off to the stream to splash like kids with excitement. When the ladies bounced into the arena the warriors suddenly halted, in wonder and admiration, hearts pounding.

The ensuing mêlée, contrasted comfortably with that highland horror; soapy soft flesh and shiny muscle under the hot African sun. The scene had colonial connotations perhaps? At any rate memorable.

Jo and I returned to our log cabin at Kitulo.

With temperatures of 30° C at noon and minus 5° C frost at dawn, and in the rainy season, ground level cloud and violent electric storms that flood the turf with rivers of light, Kitulo is a frightening place. These hostile extremes manifest themselves in the minds of African men in the form of the unearthly powers of ancestral spirits.

This fear, resulting in the absence of human exploitation has proved to be a wonderful conservation factor. The high plateau has become a palaeo ecological gem of rolling grasslands with a substrata of herbs and flowers, including carpets of pale blue Moraea irises and 45 species of large flowered terrestrial orchids, that have pre-historic origins. We identified an unrecorded partridge that flies in coveys like the English Common Grey. I made it my business to collect floral species on film.

Rainbow trout abound in the un-fished mountain streams, often weighing as much as four pounds. I believe that the trout were introduced in the 1930's, by that legendary intrepid pioneer George Rushby, who also started the Lime Works in Songwe valley, and killed the Njombe man-eating lions. I outwitted the wily rainbows each morning with my split cane angle and fly. Jo had them sizzling on the primus as the sun rose above the hill to wipe out the frosty patch that shaded log the cabin.

On the morning of our penultimate day together I was amazed to find my Jo plunging into the icy Ndumbi stream in her bikini. I again recalled Solomon's warnings about the strange effect that Kitulo had on peoples' minds.

'Hey! What's going on?' I shouted, concerned that Jo could be carried down to the waterfall that plunges 2,000 feet into Igawa basin. She swam downstream out of sight. By the time I had raced down to the lower trout pool, with a rope, she was nowhere to be seen. The mountain spirits had surely taking hold of her.

'Brian! Over here on the hill.'

From a state of anger I was stunned to see her there beautifully spread-eagled on the sward in the sun. I leapt across the stream to join her. The fright and then relief had set my blood racing. She stood up to meet me, and I gently held her soft shoulders and slid my hands up her neck gazing deeply into her eyes. Her every limb was trembling. I sensed her heart racing.

'When we are alone together in these wild places we are like one person you and I.' She whispered, 'I do love you.'

Our lips touched again with that spark of magnetic energy that strikes deep.

'Let's climb up Mtorwi and look at the world,' Jo said.

We clasped hands and climbed and climbed towards the craggy peak. Beyond the shoulder we paused for breath and took in the view over the Uwanji plateau far below us. We really were in the sky then, feeling wonderfully free, and special, and unaccountable. The grassy slope rose more gently then. The air was hot and still. I smiled to myself and shed my shorts and shirt cheekily, walking naked ahead of her without looking back. She responded behind me and by the time we reached the top we faced each other as nature intended, Adam and Eve, quite naked on that wild balcony. I tensed my muscles to withstand the thrill that engulfed me.

For all that it was in the sky, it was a secret place, and we could stand white and naked, looking across 40 miles of Africa, without fear of being seen. Jo extended her arms drawing me towards her until my pectoral muscles pressed into the warm softness of her breasts. We touched noses excitedly, and lips gently; progressively less and less gently, until Jo's knees gave way and we were on the grass in a welter of passion. We rediscovered the thrill of absolute abandonment and became overwhelmed to bursting point. Those dormant volcanic mountains upon which we lay were re-awakened in our loins.

Afterwards we lay on the turf, the mountain pressing into our backs, in a haze of joyous happiness, gazing at the scudding clouds and listening to distant tinkling cow bells.

A great eagle-sized red-tailed auger buzzard had settled on the crag above us and uttered its mewing call, ever watchful for a chance of a morsel below.

'That bird looks hungry. If I was you Brian I'd cover your floppy bonker. That bird could rob us both of a passionate future.'

The watchful auger buzzard tired of us and lifted off on a thermal.

'It's a good thing that the Jumbe Solomon isn't into binoculars,' Jo quipped with a grin, 'with us up here on his balcony.'

We felt more than ever in unison with nature in that wild volcanic world.

Chapter Fourteen

Looking for Ngualla

On the way home I called in at the United Nations Development Programme managed, Mbarali Irrigation Scheme on the edge of Usangu, near the deserted Igawa ranch house of pounding hearts. They had serious development problems; the dam that the international experts had built, had caused the Chimala River to divert its flow to one side, so that it required an expensive barrage of rock gabions to bring it back to the dam wall. The water level then rose to the planned level for the irrigation canals to function, but they were now silted up. Meanwhile many of the African tenant farmers had wisely absconded to the hills for fear of being unable to pay back their substantial loans.

The Baluchi Indians on the other hand, that had lived along the river ever since 1900, trickling water out bit by bit for their vegetable plots, were doing well and supplying Mbeya with lorry loads of onions. The FAO scheme manager told me that the Baluchis have always said that the UN scheme would not work. The UN of course, confines itself to 'expert' advice and does not listen to peasants. That reminded me of something I heard somewhere, "Noah built the Ark, the professionals built the Titanic."

After the meeting I wondered into the go-down and was astonished to discover one of my late father's Coventry Knight expensive luxury caravans collecting dust in the corner. My father had been a pioneer caravan manufacturer, after working in the small team of innovators that started Swallow Cars that became Jaguar. We recognised it at once as the model manufactured in the Warwick factory in the year of our marriage, 1948. Prior to our wedding Jo had worked in the factory offices and knew who the suppliers of parts were, so we felt the urge to rescue the old dear, a classic if ever there was one. I did not have a workshop facility of course, but I had a friend named Frank Larlham who was Clerk of the Works at PWD.

The manager would be 'delighted to see the back of it,' he said, 'take it, it's yours for free. I think it came from the Labour Government's infamous Groundnut Scheme just after the war.'

Back home we ran into two staggering parties, one was at the house of our departing neighbour Doctor Paul Jackson who had copious quantities of home made wine to dispose of, as well as, the ever popular blood red Cinzano and orange juice. The second party was at the Golf Club where Paul's Dutch wife Wilhelmina sang a sexy French song, which sparked off a can-can session. The outcome was a revolting drunken shambles. After spaghetti and chianti our, normally very formal and reserved Tukuyu Resident Magistrate Harry emerged from his shell and offered me a piece of his cheese, a great delicacy in Mbeya, on the blade of his penknife. This was true public school 'old school tie' camaraderie, I was quite taken aback.

Half the expatriate population attended Paul's surgery on his last morning, but not me. I managed to borrow a towing ball and fit it to my survey Land Rover and Frank and I set off for Mbarali at 8.0 am to collect the caravan, 100 corrugated murram miles ahead of us.

By noon we had it out in the sunlight to behold its jaded past glories. The anodised aluminium box section panelling was as good as new. Inside, the luxurious shower cubicle, cool larder, perspex kitchen units, folding double bed, upholstery and fittings, were all functional. Where the years had taken their toll on this mobile residence, was in the creaking joints of the patent interlocking sectional wall structure. This structure depended upon the capping mouldings to secure the vertical box sections in place as well as the moulded Perspex yellow roof corners, which were broken, making the whole structure unstable, rather like a barrel with loose hoops.

The only hope of towing it over the corrugations was a complex binding with ropes wrapping it like a parcel. We changed a tyre and set off at 12.30 pm, daring not to exceed 20 mph for fear of total collapse in the terrible road conditions.

An anxious Jo marshalled the help of Moony Loinburger and John Reece to go out and search for us after dark. By chance we had missed them quite near town, so I had to drive out after them in my Zodiac, at times touching 70 mph over the pot holes. After 20 miles I gave up. In the outcome it turned out that the rescue party ran out of petrol. At 4.30 am Frank set out again for a search and they all arrived back at 6.30 am, just in time for work. The old knight got his pound of flesh!

It was now the November RDC monthly meeting. They came up with the idea that Comrade Dawtrey should be appointed Manager of Matwiga Scheme, over-riding the Department of Agriculture. Regional Commissioner Waziri Juma said that he could 'fix it' with the Vice-President. I thought at the time that my 'African sandals' had come undone. It was not exactly what I had in mind.

Comrade Dawtrey's popularity further extended to another commitment. The presidential villageisation philosophy had caught on with the political types and I was required to explore a fertile area called Ngualla in Chunya District. It was said to be too remote for any other of the African members of the RDC to reach, in fact no-one seemed to know where it was exactly. I did, because I'd seen the old volcano from the air. As the world knows, where there are volcanoes there is fertile land that draws cultivators despite the risks of an eruption.

5th November: A government ban on the importation of fireworks, "in case of invoking a coup d'etat like that attempted by the Catholic rebel Guy Fawkes." Tanganyika News. British colonial education gone hay-wire? Our bonfire-night celebrations were reduced to Philip's cap gun, a barbecue, beer and thunderstorms, and what thunderstorms! It certainly made up for the lack of fireworks.

The following morning an African poacher made the mistake of offering us a leopard skin at our back door. He was soon enjoying free accommodation under Inspector Cochrane-Dyet. To quote Samson, 'Crocodile is take the skin for evidence.'

Next day, November 1963, Jo procured a British newspaper from somewhere. It stated that the Labour Government was intending to impose sanctions against RSA "in response to a request from President Julius Nyerere". We did wonder who would suffer most from this idea. Certainly not the Afrikaner government.

With rains threatening I needed to find Ngualla while the valleys were still crossable. With our children now at school in far away places of Tanganyika, Jo and I travelled everywhere together and I could undertake protracted long safaris quite happily. I would be taking some of my surveyors which required two vehicles. Unfortunately that would have to include our new issue Bedford 30 cwt pick-up truck, a hazard in itself!

Back in camp at Mazimbo/Matwiga social life was on the up. Doctor Don Curry the Provincial Medical Officer appeared in camp. He toured the district occasionally and viewed it as an opportunity to pursue his hobby of butterfly collecting. It was a pleasant surprise and we enjoyed walking forest paths in search of his quarry with large nets. Apparently leopard droppings are high in protein and attract exotic species, which as the doctor put it, 'gather like Yanks round a burger bar.' Near the village the children followed us excitedly, thinking that we must be starving. Don left for Chunya 'as happy as a sand boy' with wadges of envelopes containing folded, squeezed, glamorous specimens.

Tobacco seedlings were now showing in the nursery under the supervision of Tobacco Officer Dreisson, the 'affable Dane', who arrived with the DAO. We spent the day in the tobacco trials nursery, and got drowned in a heavy downpour. Two more visitors turned up, Robert Ives the Tsetse Officer and Tim Smith our VSO on his new BSA Bantam donated by Oxfam. Alexander Maki was running out of cocoa, his welcome-guest special.

I took Tim with us on an expedition to find a crossing point over the Lupa River, in readiness for our expedition to find Ngualla. I had hoped to show him 'game' or at least a guinea fowl for the pot, but saw neither bird nor beast all day. We even tried to catch a fish in the swollen river without success. We did find a rotten bridge which, after probing with knives, we decided had a hard core that might support a vehicle.

We met a hunter with a bicycle, carrying a gabori which is a typical home made muzzle loading gun that fires smoky old fashioned low pressure black powder. Since these guns were made from pipes stolen from the PWD culverts and bridges, they cannot withstand high explosive charges. The hunter had to get close to his quarry for any chance of success. I had some respect for their skill, and such men who hunt only for the pot pose no threat to conservation despite breaking the law. He told us that 'the bridge was built years ago by the Western Rift Exploration Company working for De Beers, to reach an airstrip near Ngualla.' We were on the right track! I enquired, 'did they find any diamonds?'

'Sijui, lakini, walivumbua pembe!' Don't know, but, they discovered ivory!

That evening with so many guests in camp, Jo fell to opening our reserve tin of corned beef, followed by 'Dakota cheese' and wow! Coffee. For background music we had a deafening chorus of cicadas, aroused by the rains, Alexander amused us by telling us about his tribe, and that he was black, like all his people, whereas the other surveyors were all brown. Well, in the firelight all we could see was the whites of their eyes.

He told us a remarkable story about his young son who contracted polio. Mbeya Hospital said that there was no cure for polio, so when Alexander got leave he took the boy home to Lake Victoria and consulted the local mganga. After a substantial sum of money had changed hands he began working on the boy with psychology and herbal remedies. 'My boy is now at secondary school and plays all sports. He is cured.'

We wished that Don Curry had stayed behind to give us his opinion.

We loaded the 'dreaded' Bedford pick-up with camping gear and a good steel tow rope for our Land Rover to pull the Bedford out of soft spots. I could have gladly used it to strangle those stiff necks in the ministry who wasted public funds like this, without any comprehension of the nature of our work.

We followed the winding hunter's track through miombo woodland for hours, Jo and I in silence, the African staff behind talking interminably, as ever. The atmosphere in the Land Rover cab grew more oppressive with the windows closed against tsetse flies. Our slow speed was perfect for their homing-in instincts and our warm engine giving off that infra red signal that they instinctively use to track their warm blooded prey. Inevitably we gave in as the sun rose, opened the windows and the flies swarmed in.

The track was ten feet wide, demanding constant concentration to avoid clipping tree trunks, even with our wing mirrors folded back. At mile 25 we descended into an mbuga and plunged into a great herd of black buffalo. The astonishment was mutual, my camera clicked in the panicking pandemonium of grunts, dust, steam, and the engine roar from violent reversing.

It was so easy to loose the track amongst the trees. To do so would have been disastrous especially with the Bedford having such a limited steering lock. Miombo is really like a featureless desert, we soon learned to stop as soon as a doubt arose and cast around on foot. Even if one came upon a stream there was no way of knowing which stream and whether to follow it. The hunter had told me that there was a stream running by Ngualla village so that sooner or later we hoped to find the right one and follow it.

We put another ten miles on the clock and came upon another mbuga. There were fresh elephant balls everywhere. Instead of excitement and reaching for the camera, there was alarm. Africans greatly fear elephants. We had no room to manoeuvre amongst the tree trunks. The surveyors fell silent and Okera moved down a gear to reduce engine noise as we crept forward, eyes everywhere. Ten minutes later we relaxed and the chat started again.

As the sun rose relentlessly above us I became anxious that we might be following one of those hunting tracks that leads nowhere. Jeff Jefferies, manager of the Lupa Tinga Tinga Farm told me about these local antelope hunter tracks, 'For God's sake don't get on the wrong track or we'll never see you again, there's no way of us ever knowing that you need rescue.'

Then unexpectedly we hit a river, 'My God is this the Lupa River? If it is then we've turned a full circle!' I turned to Jo, 'No, this river is much narrower and deeper than the one Tim and I saw the other day. Let's go on.'

Alexander shouted, 'Bwana, I think this is the Kikamba River. It will take us to Ngualla.'

'Good. Which way upstream or down stream? That is the question.' We were feeling much happier now.

Two wart hogs up-tailed and bolted upstream in a shining armour of wet mud, 'Let's assume that they would bolt away from human habitation and head down stream. Okera! What does your milometer say?'

'Forty five Sir.'

'Is that all ! ' Jo exclaimed as we set off down stream, 'it's taken us all day.'

We reached a flat open area that prompting Alexander to suggest a bit of tree climbing, 'if we are on the right rack Sir, we'll see smoke from cooking fires at this time of day.'

He was right, but it was some way off yet. We set off again, relaxed now.

Suddenly we found ourselves amongst a herd of frenzied elephants and reversing madly, gear box screaming, praying that the Bedford could do the same otherwise were in for a collision. The matriarch came for us in fury, head on. She must have been doing about 25 mph to our 15. Perhaps it was our screaming gear box that resembled an elephant? Then why I don't know, she turned and fled back to her fleeing herd of trumpeters. By now they were amongst the trees, trunks aloft and guards posted in a 'defensive square'. We could feel hearts pounding as we began to move forward again very cautiously.

Finally, after half an hour a small village was spotted, beyond a deeply incised stream, and there in the background was the Ngualla volcano looming skywards and cloaked in trees. The old wooden bridge was suspect and so we parked the vehicles. I climbed all over it probing with my penknife like a building surveyor. Everywhere was soft, 'the question is, will it be sound further in? Probably yes.' I declared sagely. I was alone in my optimism and no-one was prepared to accompany me in the vehicles. To cross or not to cross, that was the question.

I left it undecided as we all set off on foot to meet the village headman. His name was, apparently, Samuel, and he greeted us warmly. He was bare foot, elderly, tall and black, to quote Alexander's definition of colour, quite good looking, with gleaming happy eyes and flawless, though not particularly white, teeth. He was wearing civilised apparel for a villager, a torn vest and pot-holed trousers, but imposingly dignified for all his tatters. Samuel ordered little crouchy stools for himself and Alexander and 'proper' wooden chairs for Jo and I. Enamel mugs of drinking water followed extensive lengthy greetings and hand clapping and enquiries about families and the misfortune of having to work, accompanied by vigorous hand shaking and clasping of thumbs. There was great curiosity about the government registrations of our vehicles, were we game guards? Or tax collectors? But they were dumfounded that we had a white woman with us.

Curious village women gathered on the perimeter in increasing numbers, laden with babies and trailed by swarms of children. The air hummed with news and views. I knowingly pointed to the red soil under our feet and declared, 'this fertile soil is our business here. The Regional Commissioner sent me,' I explained with Alexander doing the translation, 'to look for fertile land to grow maize to help "feed the nation". I explained that if Samuel and his people were agreeable I could draw up a plan to allocate some of this fertile land for farmers to come here from other tribes, especially Wanyakusa, who are short of land in their area.'

This was a very tricky suggestion and I tried to deal with it politely. The outcome seemed favourable. Samuel said that he would welcome more people, and would give all the help he could to the surveyors. I had the feeling that I was being shown trust, which was probably why I was sent rather than an African Officer.

'Would his people receive payment as labourers?' Samuel enquired gently.

'Oh yes. I need men to dig soil pits and cut lines through the forest.'

The surveyors asked around about the bridge, how long had it been since a vehicle had passed that way? The old men seemed reluctant to say. A younger man volunteered the information that some Afrikaners had come that way about 20 years ago.

The termites had been busy on the wood for 20 years plus! A perilous venture indeed and Driver Okera was the first to decline to drive across, 'I've got a wife and family Bwana' etc.

Headman Samuel straightened up, and with a bold sense of leadership declared, 'I'll come with you Sir!'

'Thank you Samuel .... Twende.'

In short, the bridge held. Samuel and I were left trembling over a cup of weak sweet tea in a tin mug, Jo too. 'Topless' village women again gathered in timorous curiosity and whispered to their naked children to keep a safe distance. Later an old man drew near to shake my hand. In broken English he said that he had not spoken to a white man since the war. He said that he had been a soldier in the German Army of the Deutsche. In astonishment I said, 'You mean the First World War?' He looked surprised, and asked 'has there been another war?'

In the evening the village women gathered round our tent pointing, chattering and handling Jo's hair in obvious amazement. They sat with an air of permanency that irritated us. We hated nosiness about our ways and private thoughts. They chattered and giggled, and squabbled over anything discarded during the cooking process. Bolder women approached on hands and knees and fingered everything. As explorer Capt. Elton said in 1877 "their petty annoyances are innumerable". To make matters worse Jo forgot that our camp chair required one to plump down into it and lean back quickly otherwise it collapsed. She ended up in an undignified heap and became the centre of a scrimmage of giggling, coarse, breast swinging, perspiring women, resolved to assist her. That did it; we decided to strike our camp and take it up the hill onto the side of the volcano on the morrow, away from it all.

Samuel came to our rescue and drove the women away with a big stick. We offered him a can of lager beer after which he declared that he preferred the village pombe, so that we feared then that he would return with a pot of it. Instead he returned with an unusual guest of some mature years. He was accompanied by a handsome tame leopard. His name was Fundi Matatu. He was as black as the buffalo that crippled him, and had strong features with demanding facial scars. He laid down his crutch and told us in broken English how he'd always lived close to animals and understood their minds. Samuel told us that he was much revered in the community as a hunter and an animal expert. As a young man he had been trapped by a herd of buffalo in tall grass 'not far from here', he said, and had been terrified. I later had the ill fortune to appreciate fully his feelings. He explained how he had wounded a buffalo bull with his gabori and it came at him. All he could do was to hang on to the bull by clasping hands round his neck to avoid being trampled to death. The bull tossed his head this way and that until he was flung off into some bushes, where he lay still, bleeding and silent. The creature left.

Fundi Matatu realised then that he had a hole in the side of his face with his teeth protruding through, a dislocated shoulder and a torn muscle. He recovered very slowly with the help of the village mganga but never recovered the full use of that arm.

That was not the end of the story, though it was the end of my lager. He told us how he later had a close encounter with a nursing lioness. His pals ran but he stumbled and she grabbed him by the other shoulder. He was then dragged, unconscious to her den. When he came round with the lioness lying across his chest her cubs were chewing away at the calf muscle of his right leg. Suddenly his pals returned and attacked the lioness with spears. 'They plunged thirteen spears through her body.'

The British District Commissioner took him to Mbeya hospital where the doctor amputated his leg. Fundi was full of praise for the DC's concern and prompt help, 'in fact it was the DC that saved my life.'

I gathered that the villagers cultivated his shamba for him while he enthrals the children with his adventure stories about wild animals, and his pet leopard that protects him every where he goes.

From our tent on the foothills of the volcano, we had a view over the roof of the miombo forest canopy for hundreds of square miles below. There is something about elevation that inspires the imagination, as was the case at Kitulo, what the Americans would term an "overview" of the world. The fleeting white cloud puffs in the blue sky, reminded us of spring in Norfolk. The silent clear air and the world of tree tops seemed to me to invoke an atmosphere of expectancy. Of what? Destructive progress? I thought of how this world might have been three million years ago, pending the arrival of that two legged species, Australopithecus followed by Homo.

Aircraft never passed that way, the silence was deep, broken only occasionally by the distant sound of children at play in the village. My survey staff disliked being in remote places like this because of their Bedford truck getting stuck time and again, and the fear of contracting the deadly sleeping sickness. Jo and I were, however, quite in love with Ngualla volcano, or was it volcanic love making?

The soil survey work progressed well. The 6 foot deep soil pits were scarlet red, quite photogenic. Jo sat by each pit in turn under the umbrella with her clip board, whilst I described the red soil profile.

157

Back at the tent that evening our beloved camp site suffered a traffic hazard; columns of vicious biting siafu ants. Relentlessly unstoppable, armed to the teeth, they had taken over our tent. Samuel wisely advised us to 'go back to work and forget it, at the end of the day they'll all be gone.' He was right. When we returned the site was swept clean as a whistle by the ants. The hygienic impact pleased Jo.

After the next sweltering day I decided to turn 'hunter' for the evening and vowed to get a guinea fowl or two for supper. I had heard their noisy chatter up in the caldera as they came down for water at the spring. I set off striding uphill with my .22 rifle, alone. After a mile or so I came upon a giant fig tree and a beautiful pool. The black magnetite rock by the pool was polished and gleamed like a Victorian grate, which at first intrigued me and then alarmed me. What animal was it that drank at this pool so frequently that the rocks were polished by their bodies?

I did not have to hide long in the six foot tall grass nearby to have my curiosity fulfilled. Beneath the evening chatter of distant approaching guinea fowl, I sensed a low pitched rumbling, growley sound. It was not in one place, it was all over the hillside amongst the tall grass and rocks, invisible, but certainly buffalo. As dusk fell in the caldera, the atmosphere changed from the blissful tranquillity that lulled the senses of this macho guinea fowl hunter, to that of a fearful fleeting short trousered man, running down hill at full speed.

Miraculously two giant black buffalo bulls weighing at least a ton apiece, stepped out from nowhere right in my path, not 20 yards ahead, blocking my escape with broad wide shining black horns. They were massively forbidding. They had the spiritual support of a hundred wives in the tall grass and were not in any mood for compromise. I decided to retrace my footsteps back uphill at some speed, and to find a tree, like King Charles II, in which to hide. The only trees around were acacia thorn trees!

My lengthy sojourn in the branches turned out to be a painful one, with two inch hypodermic needles finding a fresh posterior puncture site with every shift of position. I sat still as a statue in the now cold moonlight, fearful of a slip to my death. The black beastly mass below persisted for hours, I could feel their warm breath, taste the aroma of heaving meat, and hear their low grumbles as they queued impatiently for a drink.

I decided to have a go at scaring them off. I was able to fire ten rounds rapidly and create quite a noise within the echo-chamber of the caldera. General commotion ensued with much snorting and growling and crashing about in the tall dry grass. Then the panic subsided but the 'window of opportunity' did not emerge The herd were now centred round the tree breathing heavily, uttering short conversational grunts of anxiety and perplexity, as though to say to each other 'where is that dratted flea of a white man? He must be crushed.'

The hours crept slowly by. It was as though this was their 'resort' of leisure. Well chosen I supposed. In the small hours I plucked up the courage to jump down and run like a rabbit. Jo was distraught, 'hunting-for-the-pot you said, in future we'll stick to canned beans.'

Village headman Samuel fell about with mirth at hearing the drama of Bwana Pima's guinea fowl hunt. This prompted him to relate his experiences of hunting buffalo with certain white-hunters 'during the last moon'. My ears pricked up. He told me that, they first came during the last rainy season and employed his whole village, and Lukwati village to the south. They cleared the old air strip in the forest, 300 yards long for their ndege, which is Swahili for bird meaning aeroplane. 'I was employed as a tracker,' he continued, 'and to begin with it was good, but they killed so many animals, that we were sick of killing; kongoni [hartebeest], nyati [buffalo], punda milia [zebra], and tembo [elephant]. We Africans kill what we need for our people to eat. These men have powerful weapons, and they use their ndege to find the nyama and then kill, kill, kill. We were not happy. Why do they need so much nyama? Could you, Sir, talk to the Bwana Nyama in Mbeya about this?'

'No need' I responded with a smile, 'look.' I dug in my tunic pocket and pulled out a small wallet, 'This is my warrant.' Alexander read and translated firmly, 'Brian Dawtrey is hereby gazetted by Tanganyika Government as an honorary Game Warden. This confers upon him the power of arrest and confiscation of evidence and property, of any suspected poacher. Signed by Chief Game Warden.'

'Bwana. I heard that ndege yesterday.' enthused Samuel 'They must be here now. I've got four men with gabories. If you like I can take you there.'

I nodded thoughtfully; I was letting myself in for a serious encounter. 'OK, let's do it.'

Chapter Fifteen

Poachers, Mudd and More Mudd

'Now, Samuel, I need to take Fundi Matatu and his leopard with me. Can you find him and tell him we can carry his leopard in my Land Rover, and we'll take the Bedford for back-up and to carry any confiscated nyama for your peoples' chakula. Also we'll take two government surveyors as witnesses. When the hunters see two government vehicles and a leopard, they will be fearful.' The words nyama, meaning wild animals, and chakula meaning food, are synonymous.

As Samuel told us, 'There are no villages for a hundred miles, nor any vehicle tracks. We must follow the river valley to avoid getting lost.'

It was grassy and more open in the valley. After a while fresh elephant droppings put everyone on the alert in case of a sudden charge. An hour passed then Samuel shouted 'Turn right here Bwana.' Tribal Africans have an amazing geographical sense. We travelled into rising wooded ground for a short way. We were spot on, open sky and an air strip. We parked the vehicles well back and I told the drivers to come when I blew my whistle. I signalled Fundi Matatu to stay behind also. The leopard curled her lip and cursed threateningly whenever I approached Fundi.

At the edge of the airstrip Samuel and I hid behind a tree and listened intently. Nothing. We could now see a bell tent, racks of meat being smoked and a Piper Apache plane shimmering in the heat, looking so incongruous. Where had they come from?

We approached the camp cautiously. Still no sign of movement. In the tent were trophy heads of hartebeest female, the long beautiful curving horns of the rare male sable antelope, and black horns of a buffalo, again female. Since this was the breeding season I was convinced that these men were indiscriminate killers rather than bona fide hunters.

The vehicles were duly whistled up and parked in front of the plane to prevent escape whilst I peered inside the locked plane windows. There was a pair of elephant tusks of about 50 pounds each, value about my annual salary, and four high powered rifles.

'Can we load the nyama into the back of the Land Rover?' asked Samuel imploringly.

'No no. Don't touch anything, wait until we've checked their licences, otherwise they could charge us to court for theft.'

Time dragged by slowly. My men lay in the shade. I thought about Jo snoozing in camp, feeling glad that she had stayed behind. Suddenly we were alerted by distant voices. Everyone grabbed a gun or a branch of wood and listened. At first nothing, then, at the north end of the airstrip, a group of men with binoculars trained on the camp were there. We approached them as they came forward so as to appear positive. The hunters were four white men dressed in khaki shorts tunics and broad brimmed hats, followed by a few porters, from where? I wondered. 2 carried tusks, 2 with pangas and axes, used for cutting the tusks out of their victim's face, were carrying elephant feet.

I felt anger rising. I thought, 'they'd just better have elephant licences!' I signalled Fundi Matatu near the tent to tree his leopard, which he did. The hunters, having no weapons, strode up to the bell tent with aplomb. The porters gathered together clutching their pangas and axes, whilst my men circled them. The leader, an older white man with sun tanned face and piggy eyes, chin pointing upwards, said loudly in a heavy Afrikaans accent, 'Something we can do for you boys?'

The atmosphere was tense and the bon homme manner of the leader was not reflected in the faces of his retinue. I spoke plainly but with a smile, 'My authority card. I am a Game Warden doing a routine check on hunting and gun licences.'

'Jesus. My congratulations on getting out into this God forsaken hole. British grit I'd say by the accent,' he said somewhat gratuitously. My face straightened. 'I have an elephant licence of course, and topi, sable, buffalo. They're in the tent. I'll get them.'

Alexander followed him and watched him intently thinking he might pull a hand gun from amongst the boxes. However he came out smiling broadly and obviously feeling he had these amateurs taped. 'Here you are, all honky dory.'

I scrutinised them carefully. 'Good. Just one thing bothers me. The horns are female and it's out of season. And then there's the matter of tusks. Your licence is for one elephant. Can't say I've heard of an elephant with four tusks, not since the Jurassic?'

'How do you mean four?' His face became stern, almost fierce.

'In the plane, two more?'

'Oh.hh… They're from outside, didn't get them here. Northern Rhodesia.'

'I see. You imported them? How about Customs? Do you have an export permit?'

There was a pregnant pause. And then 'Ah … must be in the plane. Let's go and look.'

Fundi was standing by me, 'Call your chui.' No-one had noticed her in the tree. Pandemonium broke out when she leapt down. Fear struck like lightening as they scattered in all directions. She made straight for us and the white hunter, who turned deathly pale but felt he could not run as long as we stood our ground. Fundi stroked and petted the leopard. I shouted 'It's OK! The leopard is tame. Quite harmless. As long as you don't threaten her.'

The surveyors were busy translating to the fearful labourers. Fundi, Alexander and I reached the plane and keys were duly produced by a trembling hand. The big man took a deep breath and recovered his composure.

'Right, I'll climb in and get the permits.'

He reappeared clutching a large piece of paper that looked to me more like a flight chart, then sharply from under it he produced a 9 mm Mauser elephant hunting rifle and cocked it. His face had recovered its brown, almost red, complexion and his eyes seemed red either from fury or from reaching over the seats for the rifle. His blood pressure was that of a drinking man. 'Right!' he said pointing the weapon straight at us, 'Bwana Game, you put your pea shooter down on the ground. … Gently now.' He then shouted 'Don't anybody move or you'll have a hole in you the size of a football. We're moving out.' He shouted to his men in that eerie dialect, 'Bring the trophies. Leave the meat. Quick about it now!'

The three white men plunged into the tent and came up with their arms full of horns and heads. Suddenly one of the African hunters gained confidence and flew at Samuel with his panga, swinging it wildly. Just then a half inch lead ball struck the assailant in the chest. He fell back and lay still as blood pumped out. Our villager had saved Samuel's life with his gabore, but aroused the Afrikaner to retaliate. 'Bloody Kaffir' he muttered and took aim steadily at our villager. He took the first pressure on the two pressure trigger. The second trigger pressure sent the bullet up into the trees in an explosion, not only of powder but of leopard fury. It was as though the leopard was suddenly the Devil incarnate. The three white hunters approaching rapidly were paralysed at the sight, dropping their trophies, and standing like open mouthed statues, as their leader went down heavily under the weight of the leopard. He was unable to scream at the intense pain of claws deep in his shoulder muscles with his throat clamped shut by long fangs. He struggled, raising dust, to no avail.

His last few minutes were a struggle to find a vulnerable point for a fist to strike the animal, but the evolutionary process has made leopards pretty well invulnerable. I picked up my .22 rifle and stuck the nozzle into the neck of the Afrikaner.

'Shall I finish you with my pea shooter? It'll be kinder.'

The bulging eyes turned towards me seemingly unrepentant. 'I'll let you live. Don't want to be charged with creep-slaughter. Fundi, call her off, now. Good girl, leave him. I think he's got the message. Good girl.'

I was not sure whether she could be persuaded to release that throat in time, and spoke calmly and kindly to her. It worked, and the victim heaved for breath. That was a relief for me really. I returned with Fundi and the leopard at his side to address the other white men who stood their ground but were whiter than just white. They knew that they couldn't make a dash for it.

'You brave young men can carry these trophies and the tusks to my Bedford pick up. As a gesture of goodwill I will deposit them with the Game Department in Mbeya for you to collect. Your rifles will be there too. Alexander! Collect the rifles from the plane please. The villagers at Ngualla will love you for the meat, so you haven't come off too badly really. No injuries either ... yet. Except for the Bwana huko that is. Hope one of you can fly the plane; your boss needs a hospital. There's one in Mbeya. Ask for Doctor Curry. Then ask for David Ansty's office that's where the trophies will be - eventually.

We helped shocked Samuel to the Land Rover and set off for Ngualla, everyone grinning like Cheshire cats, and licking their lips in anticipation of nyama.

Ngualla is 500 feet lower than Matwiga and that much hotter. Jo was dripping with perspiration as well as curiosity as to our adventures and trophies.

I suggested a swim in the caldera. She accepted at once despite my narrow escape with the buffalo up there, 'Well,' she said 'lightening never strikes twice in the same place does it.'

It was perfect, the giant fig tree for privacy, deep cool clear water - no bilharzia, solitude. 'Lots of fig leaves to hand if the odd hunter should pass this way.'

We lay au-naturel on the black shiny rock to dry in the evening sun. 'Can you sense the magnetism Jo?'

'Bragging again!'

'No, No, I don't need to. I mean this rock, its magnetite.'

'Look, Adam, this is not the place. You seem to be obsessed with making love in volcanic mountains. This caldera is too popular at sundown. Listen to those guinea fowl there must be hundreds on their way down here for their sundowners. Not to mention the odd lion and the odd hundred plus buffalo.'

Dawn always brings a chill mist over the forest canopy, and that strange booming hornbill reminding us of the Norfolk reed beds and the booming bitterns. The sun rose red to inflame the red hues of the Brachystegia trees in their spring flush. There were green leaves too shining in their newness, curling in the slight morning breeze. The eerie silence was broken when the sun warmed the village and the children begin their ding-dong chatter. Another hot day in the red soil pits lay ahead of us.

We soon completed our preliminary survey and our thoughts turned to Mbeya comforts. The night before our departure it rained torrentially and the river became impassable forcing us to seek a route directly south towards Lake Rukwa .This route was an old footpath used by the Catholic missionaries from Gua. The prospect of reaching the Outspan spurred us on to chance this uncharted route.

It was late November, warm and raining. I dedicated myself to seeking out the civil servant who had allocated us the Bedford and to drop a lump of mbuga clay in his In Tray. We set off at 9.30 am, 'steam rollering' the bushes with the Land Rover to make a passage for the Bedford.

After half an hour we were astonished to see a government-issue officer's tent lying back amongst the trees. We stopped to investigate. Sitting at a camp table covered with stones was a white man in khaki shorts and tunic, bare legs and plimsolls. As Jo and I approached I could see that he was labelling rock samples. He rose and somewhat ceremonially donned a soft hat to greet us. I was thin as a rake from perspiring such a lot but this man was even slimmer than me, and also like me, I suppose, of earnest countenance.

'How do you do, Sir. I'm Brian Dawtrey Land Planning Officer. This is Jo my wife,'

'Lucky you, if may say so.' He said doffing his hat politely, 'My name's Mudd.'

'Oh well, if you say so,' said Jo struggling to suppress a giggle, 'just joking. You look like a geologist?'

'Absolutely. Geological Surveys Dodoma. Care for a coffee?'

His collection of rocks was fascinating, and we talked a lot about the origin of those dark red soils at Ngualla, and the prolificacy of wildlife in this area. He told us that he does seven months alone in the bush, with one 'exciting day' a month in Chunya. We gained the impression that he was disinclined to chat too long as it only extended the time he would have to be in the bush.

So many young British colonial officers have done invaluable work for Tanganyika in mapping natural resources under very arduous conditions. He explained that he was replacing a colleague who was convalescing from a snake bite that he had suffered when cutting traces west of Ngualla. Apparently the boomslang was hanging in the branches and got him in the shoulder, so that he could not apply a tourniquet. He was carrying anti-snake venom serum which got him back to Dodoma, from whence he was flown to Nairobi Hospital. 'He was three months under treatment there, and returned with a hole in his shoulder muscle, in which he now carries his pencils.'

Another three and a half hours of rock and roll and we were still only 18 miles out of Ngualla, hindered by wet mud under the wheels of the Bedford, and Mudd in my ear. We came to a village called Lukwati. There was a self-help primary school built of mud, wattle and grass. The furniture was rows of timber rails set one foot above the earth floor to seat the obviously enthusiastic children. There was a loud chorus of English recitation to be heard as we paused. They were making the most of their opportunities to learn, with a dearth of facilities.

Their geography lesson was a map in the dust outside, marked with white stones, showing the district features. In the centre was a hand made large national flag. The teacher emerged to greet us. Jo and the teacher stood and talked for ages, and then addressed the pupils. Jo told them all about Ngualla and the red soils; about Kipembawe One-acre Tobacco Scheme; about Uwanji and the pyrethrum flowers that go for export to England, and about elephants;

buffalo, and tsetse flies. She said that one day pyrethrum insecticide from Uwanji would be used to kill the tsetse flies in Lukwati, and get rid of that horrible disease, sleeping sickness. We were so impressed with the childrens' enthusiasm for learning, and quite unrelated to the state of their school buildings or equipment.

The footpath became a track, luxury indeed, and in only three quarters of an hour we were talking to the White Fathers at the Gua Mission. It took great resourcefulness to survive in such a remote place, not to mention dedication. We heard that they were not alone in their desire to win souls. There was a strongly influential witchdoctor named Chikanga, who came from Nyasaland, (now Malawi), who held sway over much of the Southern Highlands as well as in his homeland.

Chikanga was a worry to politicians as well as missionaries. He enjoyed donations from the people whom he helped, because they believed him and trusted him, and to some extent feared him. The TANU Party henchmen on the other hand were, to quote the Fathers, 'fearsome liars and untrustworthy'. The fathers went on to say that Chikanga was opposed to tobacco and maize growing schemes in Chunya District and we 'should be careful, as he's dangerous'.

We were greatly refreshed by the mission lemonade, and Jo ventured to enquire of a red round faced Canadian Brother, 'How does a Brother become a Father? I've always wondered?'

He smiled and said, 'You mean you don't know how a Brother becomes a Father! Well it's simple really, by having fun with a Nun.'

The grassed over murram road from Gua towards Chunya followed Lake Rukwa on our right. It was several hours long and water tended to cross it from left to right as one would expect. That was a bad portent for the Bedford driver, and sure enough when passing a mountain on our left in the Kwimba area, called Ndutwa, the Bedford became hopelessly stuck during a cloudburst. We were not far from Rukwa Outspan by this time, so I decide to seek help from Mr Nel.

Ndutwa peak stood starkly alone in the landscape above the lake and consequently attracted local superstitions. A local mzee, meaning a senior person or old man, passing by, stopped to help us with our interminable digging and cutting timbers for making a road under the Bedford wheels. My trainee Eric, being a local man could understand his dialect and related his interesting tale of tribal custom in regard to Ndutwa. He said that the mountain was holy and felt sure that it had influenced our misfortune, especially since Ndutwa was the god of rain. It is often the case that isolated peaks attract heavy rain of course. 'The mountain,' he said, 'did not favour strangers, especially those that planned to bring many more strangers into the area.'

I gathered that this flat topped table-like mountain was revered by the Wakimbu tribe whom I suspect were the ones driven away from Lake Nyasa's fertile shores soon after Capt. Elton met their chief in 1877, where they would have understood very well the strong association with high rainfall and the mountains below which they lived at the time.

Mzee told us that when he was young the tribal elders used to strip naked to ascend Ndutwa and face the 'God of Fire on the mountain top. They carried a red cloth, to shield their eyes against being blinded, and dragged with them a slightly drugged sacrificial girl.'

Apparently the unfortunate girl was, in due course, throw over the edge of the vertical face of rock, to fall 700 feet to the glory of the rain-god, and ensure good crops. I did wonder what else they found attractive about this mountain top excursion!

Mzee assured us that the villagers considered it a great privilege to have one's daughter selected for this sacrifice, and were rewarded by having their gardens cultivated for them for a year.

We certainly made our sacrifice ... of body coolants, energy reserves, and fortitude. Still the Bedford sided with the mountain as darkness fell. What next? Jo and I made an easy decision, a night at the Outspan. Everyone piled into the Land Rover and we all churned off past Ndutwa into the night. It was an evening for ghosts, and one appeared. Silence fell in our crowded vehicle as our headlights picked up a fleeting white, giant butterfly-like creature flapping crazily like a bird in a wedding dress. It appeared and disappeared, flashing red eyes at us and trailing streamers. Okera became anxious to get the evil mountain behind us and accelerated wildly through the mud so that were thrown sideways at times in an alarming manner.

It was not far down to the lake and we were all soon fixed up for the night. In the bar Philip Nel explained that the pennant winged nightjars at this time of year grow long white streamers to attract their mates in the darkness and flap about exactly in the manner of butterflies.

The next day was Saturday, Philip Nel as ever, had the solution, an extra high lift Tanganyika jack, and some planking. I packed the surveyors off to their wives and loaded them with the game trophies. Jo had stayed behind at the hotel and apparently joked with Christina Nel that she was looking for a big strong man to go off the rails with. That decided me to stay overnight again and limit her choice to, White fathers, 60 something year old Philip Nel or Digger Dawtrey. She settled for going off the [bar] rails with me and later acquiesced to a skinny dip with the hippos and tiger fish before being rescued by her husband. Another passion of ours was elephants. West of Gua, the Provincial Game Warden had informed me, was where a large number of elephants gathered at this time of year. The rains would soon make access impossible, so, reckoning that I was entitled to a day's extension to the weekend Jo and I agreed to turn back and head for the River Rungwa valley, via Gua, our appetite for adventure unabated.

Jo's leg ulcers from Ngualla tsetse fly bites were responding well to gentian violet. I was hoping that she would develop a resistance, as one sometimes does with malaria.

I explained to Christina Nell that we were off on an adventure into the unknown in search of elephants and she sympathetically offered us the loan of her cook-boy, Sam.

Chapter Sixteen

Rungwa Elephants

En route to Gua we saw only one vehicle, a small motor cycle chugging along beneath the flowing white robes of Father Pierre. He explained to us that this was the only transport that he could pick up and carry round the muddy spots. He advised us that we had a daunting 70 miles to go to the Rungwa River and there wasn't a road after Gua.

Beyond Gua Mission was well into the designated Sleeping Sickness Area, rarely visited. The roadway degenerated into a bush track. We met a man pushing a wheel barrow loaded with a man lolling in it. We enquired the way and then asked about his pal. He replied balefully, '…aah ... amekufa,' he has died. He promptly trundled off towards Gua Mission. How aptly a dead body fits into a wheel barrow, doubtless he ran a small undertaking business with his unique one-wheel hearse.

At mile ten after Gua we drove into an impassable valley. We had 60 sore bottom miles on the clock since the Outspan. We happily left the Land Rover in the village nearby with strict instructions for our driver Okera Mwakajinga to meet us there on Monday.

I warned him, 'If you are not here Okera, I shall be calling for that wheelbarrow!'

I shouldered my .22 rifle, more for vanity than safety, since our enemies were more likely to be buffalo hiding in the thickets than marauding guinea fowl, and began the long trek. Following footpaths roughly parallel to Lake Rukwa, in semi-shade, we plodded on for hour after hour, swatting tsetses, slushing across mbugas, avoiding dense thickets.

At 2.0 pm we came upon recent elephant droppings in dense scrub. We now felt the need of eyes in the back of our heads. At 4.30 pm we stopped for a drink. Sleeping in the bush now seemed a prospect and we pressed on hard, passing through a village where we noticed that they had killed a buffalo. After a while we decided that we should have bought some of that meat to sustain us, and sent Sam back to 'buy some nyama and catch us up later'.

We followed an elephant trail through dense forest until 6.0 pm. The dung balls were dry on the surface and wet inside, suggesting that the herd must be still about 24 hours ahead of us. I guessed that we had come about 10 miles from the Land Rover and were feeling 'fit to drop'. Another small family of huts was a welcome sight. The shamba owner appeared and greeted us extremely hospitably. His name was Jirodi. He produced sugar cane, and later, 'senday'. This turned out to be a cool delightful drink made from bananas. At first we were dubious about tasting it, but thirst overwhelmed us, and then, 'hold us back!'

We chatted for a while with the family, whose friends gathered from near and far when they heard that we were 'looking for tembo'. That word always draws curiosity.

We had planned to move on further that night but we were too exhausted. Our excuse to stay was that a man said he'd heard tembo around that day about noon. We declared, thankfully, 'OK. We'll go after them tomorrow,' and began gathering dry banana leaves to make a bed. We were given two mats by Jirodi. A fire was made for us, and we roasted two green bananas. Then Sam appeared, grinning from ear to ear in anticipation of a feast of buffalo meat. I told him, 'go and look for some eggs while we slice this meat up for grilling'.

The village headman, called Usagara, sent a man off to find a lamp for us and some tea, mugs, and 'monsoon capes for tomorrow'. It was a kind gesture and we agreed. Usagara made the tea, as usual weak and sweet, but in our state it tasted marvellous. We could hear Sam doing a deal with eggs behind the hut. Africans don't eat eggs; of course, they prefer to leave them to become meat, which is sound bush economics. A good deal was soon in evidence. They wanted two cents each, Sam refused to pay such an 'extortionate price', but in the end he did so.

Dinner was good; hard boiled eggs; roasted sweet potato; a cup of tea; roasted banana and barbecued nyati, which Jo declined, couldn't think why? At 10.0 pm we drew lots for sleeping positions. I got the outside! I lay on half a mat and wrapped the other half over me.

We were thankful when the sun warmed the air at dawn, and whilst brewing tea and chewing sugar cane 'the spotters' went out to look for spoor. There was a foot print measuring six feet in circumference! Which must have been made by an elephant standing about twelve feet at the shoulder, weighing probably six tons. We were soon off across country, spurred on by the prospect of the biggest elephant we had ever seen. The chatter at the huts faded away behind us. After walking for three hours at a three mph pace, half the pace of an elephant, we met the sprawling River Rungwa and set off up stream.

Soon we came across the herd, not the usual but a massive gathering scattered over the landscape. There was an atmosphere of social occasion, an annual gathering of the herds perhaps, to celebrate the start of the rainy season and the emergence of fresh leaves.

There was much to-ing and fro-ing, frisking, mud wallowing and trumpeting. Baby elephants were actually sliding down muddy banks, whether by accident or design was hard to tell. The great panjandrum whose footprint we had found stood powerfully central with the younger herd bulls gathered round him in the valley bottom. A gathering of clans rather than an Olympiad of warriors.

This was another world, a dynamic, pre-historic one. Jo whispered in my ear, 'I do believe it's some kind of elephant jamboree. Just look at the family in that mud hole over there. Have you got your camera ready, take a picture of them... chocolate elephants! Nothing like mud for cooling the blood.'

Elephants were everywhere, dotted amongst mutilated trees, on every knoll, in every creek, uncountable hundreds, fearlessly going about their daily family busyness. We felt privileged to find ourselves part of a scene of twenty million years of antiquity. Crouching there on a small hillock we were awe struck and a little bit fearsome. We wouldn't stand a chance if the wind changed.

We noticed that they were very tactile; adults greeting their young by stroking them whilst teenagers pressed heads together or curled trunks like a hand shake. Mum's disciplined their youngsters by whacking them with their trunks or kicking. Mouth touching seemed common amongst all ages.

We became aware of an orchestra of acoustic sounds; trumpets were accompanied, in a high state of arousal, spreading ears and the ripping up of bushes. Clarinets screamed delight when meeting old friends, and the background to this cacophony of bellowing, screaming, and trumpeting, was a constant infra-sound of rumbling drums that carried for miles through the woodland. This rumbling was also the music of courting couples that attracted any distant male in musth for that fleeting four days every two years. With a gestation period of 22 months and a calving interval of four years the males must have learned how to cope with frustration in their long lives, of some sixty years. Certainly such longevity has produced good memories, so essential to finding food and water sources over vast distances. I have read that the elephant brain is four times larger that a human whilst their temporal lobes, responsible for memory, are much larger too. Indian elephants are known to remember 30 to 100 commands. Compare that to your pet pouch.

Elephants travel constantly and use their long trunks to follow scents on the ground. They are the mega herbivores of the eco-system, creating open areas for so many other creatures to utilise. Their only serious enemy is man, though buffalo bulls can be cantankerous and lions a threat to the calves. I have also heard of elephants fleeing from attack, returning to rescue a comrade stuck in a swamp. Crocodiles have been killed by elephants who pick them up by the tail and thrash them against the ground.

I am not sure whether elephants sleep, they seem to be like New Forest ponies which snooze standing up. We saw an elephant break a branch and use it as a back scratcher. A tool user!

Jo had been studying the activities of the babies, 'I read somewhere that their babies weigh 200 pounds at birth, and have teething problems six times over! The mind boggles. They are cuddling babies not just their own, but any retrieved from amongst the forest of legs. Imagine a harem of twenty, three ton wives, Brian, servicing their needs would be a career in itself.'

'Hey. Look down there. After their bath they are powdering themselves by blowing trunks full of white kaolin dust under their arms, tummies and ears, and over their backs. They've got their own brand of talc; Elephant Heaven.'

At 2.0 pm we decided that we should beat a retreat back to the banana shamba.

Back at the village they enquired why we were not shooting for meat. 'We are very hungry.' They lied. I knew better than to try and explain the ethics of a camera safari to 'bush people', and simply replied that we had yet to eat the remaining buffalo meat. Usagara lent us his lamp for the night.

Monday dawned with Jo in good shape except for those tsetse bites. She entertained the villagers with animated stories about her experience as an elephant tracker. Sam fixed us up with a good breakfast, and we set off in good spirits with fifteen miles of 'footing' ahead of us. We made two brief stops, one for cane sugar at a village, and then to accept the goodwill gift of a live chicken from a village headman. Concerned to reach my office the next day, I would not agree to Sam's pressure to cook the chicken, despite our hunger.

At 3.0 pm we met Okera who announced that he'd lost the Land Rover keys, doubtless hoping to stay another night, so I connected the battery to the coil and off we went, reaching Rukwa Outspan at 7.0 pm. We were absolutely starving and numb with fatigue, a feeling that Philip Nel had obviously anticipated, for he had the bath water piping hot, with food and beer ready for Sam and Okera. Jo and I bathed together blissfully, and powdered each other with kaolin powder, our own brand of Elephant Heaven.

Chapter Seventeen

Forward Control

Back at the office I received a telegram from HQ in Dar es Salaam: KIPEMBAWE TOBACCO SCHEME CANCELLED STOP NO FUNDS STOP AGDEV.

Any good 'permanent and pensionable' civil servant would bow out at such news, with an MBE for obedient service to the public in mind, but Jo and I had made huge sacrifices and we were not going to be tranquillised by centralised stuffiness. I sowed a grain of optimism for Jo, 'Kipembawe Tobacco Scheme Cancelled, means we don't have to ask them for anything, that's all. It's not their idea that's why. I've spent £4,100 on planning and I've no intention of seeing it wasted. Maybe they haven't sussed that Matwiga is in Kipembawe? Anyway it's about to take off. I've even got an expatriate manager arriving any day and some settlers already selected. There'll be some red faces, you'll see.'

I think today one would call it a lack of 'joined-up government'. The expatriate community in Mbeya forecast my demise. I decided to skip the 'holy' Monthly Report ritual and keep the egg-heads at HQ guessing. I pinned my survival hopes on the RDC and its local political types. 'They'll ring-fence me when the time comes.' I prophesied.

My justifiable complaining about the Bedford, over the past weeks had found a friend in the echelons of the ministry in Dar., I didn't know who but guessed it might be John English. I received a Forward Control Land Rover. What an extraordinary invention! The driver sat forward of the front wheels giving the driver a yo-yo ride in the field. The extra long chassis gave it much greater carrying capacity for surveyors and their equipment. An appointment to meet Sammy Clark the Iringa Field Officer to look at my Kitulo Wool Sheep Scheme plan, gave me the chance to try out this new vehicle. Would such a high vehicle be stable on those mountain slopes I wondered.

The poor steering lock gave me problems climbing the 56 hair-pin bends up the escarpment to that 'lost world' Kitulo, but I soon had the mature age Sammy Clark, sitting beside me busily calculating the fuel consumption so far, 'Ha … seven miles to the gallon! You'll have to carry a 45 gallon drum of petrol everywhere Brian,' he said, feeling a bit queasy with the up and down roll over the plateau.

The early rains had struck magic into those down-lands. We marvelled at the great shoals of Knipofia in the wet vales, red hot pokers in brilliant yellows and reds. The rolling banks of fine grasses were now hidden by carpets of Asters and Helichrysums. This was the time also for my favourite flower the Clematopsis. These grow in spreading clumps of single large buttercup type drooping cream coloured blooms. Sammy separated one out for my camera.

What I had taken to be rank grass was now a willowy spray of delicate pink bell like blooms borne on waving filipendulous stems. This bloom was as delicate in appearance as to seem out of place in that strident environment, a case perhaps, of beauty beguiling. I have subsequently found the name to be *Dierama pendulum*, of which some cultivated varieties are appearing at garden centres in England.

A four day holiday celebration loomed, for the union of Zanzibar with Tanganyika, to be renamed Tanzania, the zan being pronounced as in Zan-zibar. This holiday coincided with end of term and an invitation to visit my ex-elephant hunter friend Steve Stevenson who was now Warden of Rungwa Game Reserve soon to be re-designated Ruaha National Park

His camp HQ was called Mbage, situated on the Iringa end of the Usangu Plains on the bank of the Ruaha River. I had arranged for Jo to meet me in our Ford Zodiac, below the escarpment at Chimala, from whence we would proceed together to Iringa to meet all the children.

Coming down the hairpin bends in the F.C. Land Rover was more hair-raising than it was going up. If you can imagine being seated forward of the front wheels swinging round those hair-pins over a 3,000 foot drop, then you will appreciate what those girls felt like as human sacrifices being thrown over the edge of Mount Ndutwa.

Jo was suffering again with those painful tropical ulcers from tsetse flies. Her legs were painted purple with gentian violet. She assured me that she would be feeling better by the time we met the children.

We checked into the luxury of the White Horse Inn at 6.30 pm. We were welcomed by the Greek manager Sophacles, who dined with us. We discussed the frustrations of life in Tanzania, the closure of schools, public misadministration, departing expatriate skills and general lack of public funds. Our love of wild Africa always refreshed our morale, and our plan was to take the children on an exciting safari down to Steve's Mbage Camp, for a step back in time. We all agreed that an exchange of animals for people would be the perfect antidote to the stress of end of year school exams.

After discussing Kitulo Wool Sheep Scheme plan with PAO Don Muir, and meeting the other expatriate officers in the Agriculture Dept., Don Randall, Jim Moss, the aggrieved Bob Mansfield and Max Lloyd, Jo and I raced down to St Michael's and St George's School to collect Caroline for the last time. In future she would be taught at home on a PNEU correspondence course. House Mistress Mrs Wiltshire's opinion that Caroline was not an academic, came as no surprise, and she was right about, 'when given a challenge Caroline can climb mountains, and give a lead to others. She is a courageous girl, kind and popular.' Could be a description of Jo too, I thought.

We found ourselves amongst a crowd of expectant parents at the, train-less, Railway Station. It was Saturday 7th December, 1963. At 2.30 pm it all happened, the bus gasped its last with green shirted, grey hatted children hanging out of every window and the bus's ubiquitous mountain of dust mantled baggage on the roof. Philip appeared with shirt tails hanging out and hat to one side at an angle, clutching a small unclose-able suit case tied with string. Richard appeared white faced, apparently through lack of sleep at the mosquito ridden Railway Hotel in Dodoma. He was struggling with a large bundle wrapped in his 'mac' and a grip. They had departed at midnight on the fifth.

The boys were full of news for their overwhelmingly happy parents. Eleven year old Richard told us that he had won 200 marbles having borrowed the first one, a school record. That could have been a portent of years to come and was certainly a reflection of his farmer's boy initiative. He claimed another record of more dubious merit; 7,000 lines in one day. We were right to predict that Richard would become an achiever, even though he hated school.

Eight and three quarters year old Philip announced that he had won Stars for gymnastics, swimming, drawing and 'all round effort', and that he liked boarding school, which was a huge relief to Jo of course. Upon recent reflection we suspect that he said that to please his beloved Mum, knowing that she had been very distressed over their too early separation. He told us that the school was dropping French in favour of Kiswahili, which both of them were pleased about. The school was also dropping English history in favour of African history, which worried us. They knew all about Tippu Tipp, the biggest Arab slaver of all time who treated Tanganyika as his empire, until the Germans kicked him out in 1885.

A massive Sunday breakfast set the children up for adventure. School was already history, best forgotten. On our way westwards we took them to see a remarkable mission secondary school for African girls, called Tosamaganga, established in 1890 and, it is said, almost totally self supporting from the sales of embroidery done by the African girls. The Nuns said, 'Oh yes we know of you Mr Dawtrey.' and served us with excellent home-made lemonade from their own orchard. What did they mean?

Half way down the rain soaked track to the Ruaha River it grew hotter, more humid, and tsetse ridden. I was reminded of a camp fire song of my youth called Life Gets Tedious Don't It; I chanted it to my car full   "we open the windows and the tsetses swarm in, we shut the windows and we're sweatin agin."

We swatted tsetses on each other's backs, in order of seniority with Philip last. He courageously declared with obvious feeling; 'I'd rather have tsetses than mosquitoes! At least you know there's game about.'

A crocodile plopped into the river where the track ended. We had done 50 miles of rough track to reach the boundary of the 7822 square miles of the Reserve. I had figures in my head again, 'This is the home of 22,000 elephants,' I declared, 'they need 228 acres each. Human beings, in England anyway, live off one and a quarter acres per person. But humans are multiplying so fast that there is a threat to the elephants if we don't protect them like they are doing with this huge Game Reserve.'

A game guard in green uniform emerged from the shrubbery and saluted, *'Jambo Bwana Dawtrey, napende kupita mto?'* You like to cross the river?

The pontoon that Steve had rigged up was basic! Hand hauled on a chain. I enquired concernedly, *'Infasi kwa gari?'* Is it possible for a car?

'Na weza.' It can. I thought, a bit vague. *'Twende Bwana.'* Let's go, rather decided it. The game guard didn't waste words, like his master, Steve.

The pontoon only just fitted under our four wheels. Muscle power and the chain took us over and under the wooded bank opposite. We drove into Steve's camp nestling under a massive fig tree which shaded two aluminium rondavels with the roofs thatched for coolness. Behind the rondavels was a tall grass screen with a converted 45 gallon oil drum above for showering. The dining room was an open sided grass surround with one of the most magnificent views in Africa, encircled by the bustling Ruaha River which provided colour and sound to the menu. The incessant chatter of river birds accompanied by gurgling water attracted our immediate attention and the recognition of knob-nosed geese with chicks, glossy violet Abdims storks, 4ft 6" tall brown Goliath herons, Hammerkops with heads like hammers, spectacular turquoise and blue rollers and their competitors for startling colour the little malachite kingfishers and lots more.

Steve soon had us fascinated with his eternal passion for elephants. He told us that 'they have a self-service restaurant just behind the camp. There is a giant sweet-fruited Acacia albida tree and palm tree fruits for afters.' There were more elephants in Steve's bed-sitter, shelves of titles; Loxodonta this, Loxodonta that, Karamoja Bell, Record Tusks And Their Location Killed &c. His lonesome evenings were spent with Handel's Water Music, snatches from The Messiah and Scheherezade.

In the evening Steve started his generator and ran some ciné film for us; the commentary went, 'the cheeky one. There's always one in every classroom, isn't there. I call him Castor. Here he is scrumping fruit from my palm tree.'

Everyone laughed at Castor shaking the palm tree to bring down the fruit. He did it by laying his trunk vertically along the tree trunk and pushing back and forth. This had the amusing effect of peeling his tusks, alternately yellow to white, and creasing up his 'trousers' and stumpy short hind kegs. The net result was for a hefty fruit to crash down upon his head.

'Don't worry if you hear a snuffling and munching noise in the night, that'll be Castor chewing your thatch. He's a young bull; hasn't learned any manners yet, quite tame though, doesn't mind humans at all.'

After the film Philip asked 'Steve, where does your little pet dikdik sleep?'

'Under my bed. He's safe there. If anything frightens him he's inclined to run too fast across the shiny floor though. The last one I had did the splits and died. Look at his legs, no thicker than a pencil are they. He loves sausage flies. They come to the Tilley lamp in the evening, get burnt and provide a feast of hot-dogs.'

After lunch next day we drove half a mile inland to a dry sandy river bed, crossed it and drove up to Steve's airstrip. He took Caroline and Jo up in the Piper Apache to look at the herds of buffalo, zebra and elephant on the open plateau grasslands. The boys and I wandered back to the 'dry' sand river and were alarmed to find it running deep raging water. There had been no sign of rain. 'There's obviously been a cloud burst in the hills,' said Steve when they returned, 'tell you what, I'll take you boys up with your dad for a fly round and by the time we get back the river will have dropped.'

This was an experience of a lifetime for the boys. We skimmed the grass in places, hopping over ostriches and herds of eland, hartebeest, leaping impala, Grants gazelle, zebra, we had never seen or dreamed of such a concentration of wild animals, not even on the farms in Norfolk. There were lots of young about too. A great black mass of buffalo attracted our attention and we swooped down low over them causing their attendant cattle egrets to rise like a cloud of greenhouse white fly. Cattle egrets feed on the grass hoppers disturbed by the buffalo and at times ride their backs on the look out like tourists on an open bus in London.

The boys had already decided that there was only one life for them when they leave school, and they were going to persuade Dad to make a move in his work into National Parks for his next 'tour'. That turned out to be a premonition.

The sand river had dropped enough to wade across and then, to hook up a steel cable to a tree the other side, to pull the Land Rover across. Easy, although it can float off a bit, ours did!

One and a half inches of rain fell after supper followed by a steamy hot stillness. The sly hooping call of hyena made us cringe. Few animals are so repulsive round a carcass, sniggering, giggling, moaning, shrieking and screaming with eerie laughter. Distant zebra could be heard whinnying like a donkey with hiccups. That night I dreamed I had a scorpion in my hair. It must have been Castor stripping the thatch.

After a creepy night the mourning doves cooed tranquillity into the atmosphere as everything steamed in the early sun. The boys caught a ten pound barbel and only just managed to land it before an aggressive hippo asserted its rights of way in the river.

At 9.30 we were flying again, heading for the distant plateau where doubtless, explorer Captain Elton passed, to his death. There were elephants galore; tusk ivory 70 pounds a side; and a maze of tracks. This place was pre-Homo sapiens. I hoped that it would stay that way. The open plains were speckled with giraffes. We swooped this way and that, our stomachs plunging with excitement, over herds of zebra and buffalo. Then we climbed and circled high above the vast disc of dehumanised landscape, bordered by far away dark mountain ridges, threatening rain.

'Look at that black sky,' said our pilot, 'we must get back before it breaks or you'll all be stuck here for Christmas.'

'Wow! That'd be great,' exploded Phil. But that was not exactly the plan. We were due to leave that afternoon, the Zanzibar union holiday was over.

Faces were black as the sky when I explained that I had to get back to work.

'There's plenty to keep you busy here Dad,' pleaded Richard hopefully.

However the die was cast and we were soon floating across the river to the 'civilised' side, and off up the track towards Iringa. Wet sandy patches were packed with butterflies supping moisture. My mind returned to those packs of civil servants at the ministry HQ who sent hopeless telegrams to Land Planning Officers. These were more easily activated. We were cheered up as we drove homeward through clouds of golden butterflies, myriad wings like confetti at a heavenly wedding.

Our joy turned to consternation as we found ourselves facing a four foot deep gully where a culvert had been washed out in the night's rain. Caroline was the first out, staring into the abyss, sizing up the situation and considering what might be done to alleviate our predicament.

'You know what I think Dad, there's nothing for it but to fill this hole in with rocks, sand, and wood. There's no way round. What tools have you got Dad?'

Richard stepped up with a bright twinkle in his eye, 'I think we should go back, before it gets dark!'

'Don't worry I've got a spade, an axe, and a survival kit.' There was a chorus of, 'an umbrella, and a banana.'

We all pitched in, family unity at its best, facing a challenge to survive. It took us three hours. There was still a hollow of soft soil and it was necessary to rush it on the skew so as not to have both wheels of one axle in the hole at once. It was so hairy that a cheer was raised when I emerged the other side. We lived on.

It became cold with black clouds and we closed all windows leaving the tsetses to starve on the boot. We reached Iringa at 6.30 pm.

The main topic of conversation at the White Horse Inn was Kenya's

Uhuru celebrations with the Duke of Edinburgh representing the Queen. It had taken Kenya two years longer on account of problems with Mau-Mau. Jomo Kenyatta said that he "wants the White Highlands back". We gathered that British law and order and health provisions had resulted in a doubling of population every eighteen years. Hence the population of 2 million in 1897 when the Highlands were occupied by white farmers had risen to 8 million at that time. The figure in 2002 was 35 million. 'But wouldn't the voters rather have jobs on the farms and plenty to eat' someone said. 'We shall see.'

On the long drive to Mbeya we dropped in for coffee at the farm of Lady Ricardo, about 60 miles out. She runs Shorthorn cattle and has a talking red tailed parrot. The boys discovered that by creeping out of the house and knocking at the front door, the terrier would run barking his head off down the mosquito screened corridor, where upon the parrot would screech at the terrier, 'Sit! ... Rascal ... Sit!' Sending the boys into helpless fits of laughter.

Lady Ricardo owns the Igawa Ranch House of my previous chapters. She suggested that we spend the night at the Ranch House, 100 miles short of Mbeya. It would be dark by the time we reached Igawa. We thanked her and departed.

The children were beginning to comment that the hols would be over by the time we got home, so I decided to hammer on into the night. I was driving at 60 mph under headlights when a bus passed us and blanketed us with mud. I was blind for just long enough not to see the deep donga ahead, a sort of open stream crossing with concrete bottom. We plunged into it. Our heads and our loose luggage piled into the roof followed by a punch up of bottoms. I fully expected the Zodiac to assume the shape of a boomerang, but it returned as good as ever. Not so our nerves. We decided to stop at Igawa Ranch.

Our headlights swept across the low building, draped in creepers. The driveway was grassed over. No sign of life, not even a watchman. There was no rush to get out of the car either, 'Anyone know where the torch is?'

'In the boot.' No volunteers. I dragged my aching backside out of the driver's seat and found my way to the back of the house. It was a velvet black night. There was no sound but for the tinkle of water cascading from the far off Kitulo Mountains. The back door opened with a complaining creak and a tumbling shower of dust and termite clay. My torch beam wandered round the large curving lounge, over dust coated furniture, a cobweb festooned rattan cane chair, zebra skins, and a heavy mininga mahogany dining table of the dimensions that one finds in monasteries.

I went back out and called cheerfully, 'Come on in, it's OK. Bed and breakfast with wonderful views of the mountains, and there's no charge. I need the pressure lamp, and a large duster.'

'And a bunch of bananas,' someone added sarcastically. My first love; sorry second.

The hiss of the Tilley lamp somehow imbued an air of normality into a precariously unwelcoming situation. We gazed quizzically round the cavernous lounge. As our eyes became accustomed to the dark, we noticed eyes everywhere and furry faces, looking down upon our huddled group. Trophies! Benign antelopes, fierce buffaloes, a snarling lion, horns of every shape, a fossilised parade of nature's genetic miracles of evolution. The parade terminated over the bedroom door with the head of a leopard.

'I'm not sleeping in there!' erupted Caroline. Never the less she was not going to stay behind in the dark either. We all filed behind the lamp into the bedroom to watch Jo pummelling the mattress,

'Not surprised Lady Ricardo moved out. Yuk what's this, a rat's nest. Stinks. They say where there's rats there's snakes. I'd rather sleep on the lawn.'

'Trouble with that is it's going to rain.'

'Right, let's inspect the cupboards for snakes then, come on bring the lamp.'

'I'll just pop out and get my simi from the car. And the food box.' I decided.

We finally opted to sleep in the lounge under the watchful gaze of the dead and departed. 'Sleep well.' I commanded.

It was the twelfth of December. In the welcome light of dawn, we found the stream and used it for ablutions and tea water. The boys used it as a potential gold strike and began panning earnestly, 'there's something here Rich, look at this, real shiny in the bottom. You remember that Chunya story of Dad's. You never know.' So they had been listening!

They arrived at the breakfast table bubbling with enthusiasm and saucer full of the shiny gold metal. 'What do you think Dad?'

'It's beautiful, quite heavy too. One thing bothers me, if there was gold here, would the Ranch be deserted? We'll keep it for posterity.'

There was a mumbling, 'Who's posterity?'

Back in Mbeya Sally spaniel exploded with joy to see the children. She became quite uncontrollable for 24 hours and even slept in their beds to ensure that they didn't escape again without her.

Back at the office; to belie the omen of the date, the thirteenth, two lucky events; one for me and the other for a certain prisoner I knew only too well.

I thought that we had seen the last of Yahaya our troublesome ex-chainman who murdered Valentino Sebastiani and was sentenced to 18 months prison. Well no such luck, he was back. In fact the lucky one arrived in my office having benefited from The Presidential Decree on the occasion of the Union with Zanzibar granting amnesty to 250 prisoners upon promise of good behaviour. The president had, it was said, "Shown good socialist will and compassion to his people". There was a sting in the tail for the law abiding citizens, however, an increase in taxes and house rents for the employed, but an increase in wages for the poorest. 'Jambo Bwana. Good marnin Sar. I am back for the job Sar.'

As he continued to effuse grace and good mannered solicitations, my face paled with shock, and then annoyance. 'Yahaya! There is no way that I will take you back with us after what you did to Valentino, and that's final.'

His face straightened and with a look of perplexity, he said, 'But Sar. I have paid for my mistake. I am clean Sar.' I dismissed him and turned to my files for consolation.

I certainly found it there! A letter from John English advising me that the WFP, or World Food Programme, had delivered £6,000 worth of food aid for Matwiga and Oxfam were ready to move it. Wonderful news, I was gasping in wonderment and joy. There was more; "The Village Settlement Agency, a new quasi-government British aid organisation had been set up and will take over the running of Kipembawe Tobacco Scheme, including Matwiga, and will be sending a project manager, named Mervyn Hallier, up to Matwiga shortly."

I really felt that the bureaucratic monster was being tamed. I rushed home to tell Jo feeling that it had all been worth while. We decided to throw a big braii, Afrikaans barbecue, party to celebrate. We invited the whole senior officer community, including the Africans, and the local coffee farmers.

We crept into Tanganyika like mice with a mission, became warriors, conquered bureaucracy, and started a family farming scheme for thousands of common hard working folk. I say we, because; Jo, me and our three children; we had all contributed.